First World War
and Army of Occupation
War Diary
France, Belgium and Germany

16 DIVISION
Divisional Troops
Royal Army Veterinary Corps
47 Mobile Veterinary Section
19 December 1915 - 30 September 1919

WO95/1968/3

The Naval & Military Press Ltd
www.nmarchive.com
Published in association with The National Archives

Published by

The Naval & Military Press Ltd

Unit 10 Ridgewood Industrial Park,

Uckfield, East Sussex,

TN22 5QE England

Tel: +44 (0) 1825 749494

www.naval-military-press.com

www.nmarchive.com

This diary has been reprinted in facsimile from the original. Any imperfections are inevitably reproduced and the quality may fall short of modern type and cartographic standards.

© **Crown Copyright**
Images reproduced by permission of The National Archives, London, England, 2015.

Contents

Document type	Place/Title	Date From	Date To
Heading	WO95/1968/3 16 Divn Divnl Troops 47th Mobile Vet. Section 1915 Dec-1919-Nov		
Heading	16th Division 47th Mob. Vety Section Dec 1915-Nov 1919		
Heading	47th Mob Vet Sect Vol I 19b-31st Dec 1919 Jan 16 16 Div Dec 15 Nov 19		
War Diary	Arrived Haure	19/12/1915	19/12/1915
War Diary	Arrived Fouquerreal	21/12/1915	21/12/1915
War Diary	Arrived Gosnay	24/12/1915	24/12/1915
War Diary	Arrived Auchy Au Bois	01/01/1916	01/01/1916
War Diary	Auchy Au Bois	02/01/1916	31/01/1916
Heading	47th Mob. Vet. Sect. Vol. 2		
War Diary	Auchy Au Bois	01/02/1916	29/02/1916
Heading	47 M.V. Sect Vol 3		
War Diary	La Perrierre Busnes	01/03/1916	09/03/1916
War Diary	Lillers	10/03/1916	27/03/1916
War Diary	Noeux Les Mines	28/03/1916	30/06/1916
Heading	47th Mobile Veterinary Section AVC 1st. July To 31st. July 1916. Volume No.8		
War Diary	Noeux-Les-Mines	01/07/1916	31/07/1916
Heading	War Diary. 47th Mobile Veterinary Section Month Of August, 1916. Volume:- 9		
War Diary	Noeux Les Mines	01/08/1916	26/08/1916
War Diary	Haye Ecquedecques	26/08/1916	30/08/1916
War Diary	Saleux	31/08/1916	31/08/1916
Heading	War Diary 47th Mobile Veterinary Section For Month Of September Volume 9		
War Diary	Daours	03/09/1916	03/09/1916
War Diary	Morlancourt	04/09/1916	05/09/1916
War Diary	Arbre Fourche	06/09/1916	12/09/1916
War Diary	Sailly-Le-Sec	16/09/1916	17/09/1916
War Diary	Tirancourt	18/09/1916	18/09/1916
War Diary	Airaines	20/09/1916	21/09/1916
War Diary	Longpre	21/09/1916	21/09/1916
War Diary	Godewaersvelde	22/09/1916	22/09/1916
War Diary	Meulehouck	23/09/1916	23/09/1916
War Diary	Mont Rouge (M.15.d.7.3)	24/09/1916	30/09/1916
Heading	War Diary Month Of October, 1916 Volume 11 47th Mobile Veterinary Section		
War Diary	Westoutre	01/10/1916	31/10/1916
Heading	War Diary. For Month Of November, 1916. Volume XI No.47. Mobile Vety Section		
War Diary	Westoutre	01/11/1916	30/11/1916
Heading	War Diary For Month Of December, 1916. Volume 12. 47th Mobile Veterinary Section		
War Diary	Westoutre	01/12/1916	31/12/1916
Heading	War Diary For Month Of January, 1917 Volume 14 47th Mobile Vety Section		
War Diary	Westoutre	01/01/1917	31/01/1917

Heading	War Diary. For Month Of February, 1917. Volume 15 Unit:- 47th Mobile Veterinary Section		
War Diary	Westoutre	01/02/1917	28/02/1917
Heading	War Diary For Month Of March, 1917. Volume 16 Unit:- 47th Mobile Vety Section A.V.C.		
War Diary	Westoutre	01/03/1917	31/03/1917
Heading	War Diary For Month Of April, 1917. Volume. 17 Unit:- 47 Mobile Vet Section A.V.C.		
War Diary	Westoutre	01/04/1917	04/04/1917
War Diary	Westoutre In The Field	05/04/1917	30/04/1917
Heading	War Diary Volume 18 For Month Of May, 1917 Unit:- 47th Mobile Vety Section		
War Diary	Westoutre	01/05/1917	01/05/1917
War Diary	St Jans Cappell	02/05/1917	31/05/1917
Heading	War Diary. For Month Of June, 1917. Volume:- 19 Unit:- 47th Mobile Veterinary Section A.V.C.		
War Diary	St Jans Cappel M26. B.88.	01/06/1917	13/06/1917
War Diary	Merris F7.B.3.7.	14/06/1917	20/06/1917
War Diary	Godewaersvelde Q.6.c.7.7	21/06/1917	28/06/1917
War Diary	Pont Derkels Brugge B19.d.6.6	29/06/1917	30/06/1917
Heading	War Diary For Month Of July, 1917. Volume:- 20 Unit:- 47th Mobile Veterinary Section A.V.C.		
War Diary	Bollezeele	12/07/1917	25/07/1917
War Diary	Watou K5d.9.7	26/07/1917	31/07/1917
Heading	War Diary. For Month Of August, 1917. Volume 21 Unit:- 47th Mobile Vety Section A.V.C.		
War Diary	Poperinghe G14.b.3.5	01/08/1917	06/08/1917
War Diary	H17.C.3.4. Sector Kieoisstrant.	07/08/1917	07/08/1917
War Diary	Poperinghe G14.B.6.4	08/08/1917	18/08/1917
War Diary	Poperinghe	19/08/1917	22/08/1917
War Diary	Achiet Les Petit	23/08/1917	31/08/1917
Heading	War Diary. For Month Of September, 1917. Volume 22 47th Mobile Veterinary Section A.V.C.		
War Diary	Boiry. St Rictrude S14.Sheet 51B.	01/09/1917	06/09/1917
War Diary	Boiry St. Rictrude	07/09/1917	30/09/1917
Heading	War Diary For Month Of October, 1917. 47th Mob. Vet. Sec. A.V.C. Volume Number 23		
War Diary	Boiry St Rictrude Sheet 51 B S14.C.6.4	01/10/1917	31/10/1917
Heading	War Diary For Month Of November, 1917. Volume:- 24 47th Mobile Veterinary Sec. A.V.C.		
War Diary	S.14.C.6.4 Boiry St Rictrude.	01/11/1917	09/11/1917
War Diary	Boiry St Rictrude	10/11/1917	30/11/1917
Heading	War Diary. For Month Of December, 1917. Volume:- 25 47th Mobile Veterinary Section A.V.C.		
War Diary	Ruyal-Court	05/12/1917	05/12/1917
War Diary	Boiry. St. Rictrude	02/12/1917	04/12/1917
War Diary	Villers-Faucon	07/12/1917	31/12/1917
Heading	War Diary. For Month Of January, 1918. Volume 26 Unit:- 47th Mobile Vety Sec. A.V.C.		
War Diary	Villers-Fancon	01/01/1918	31/01/1918
Heading	War Diary. For Month Of February, 1918. Volume:- 27 47th Mobile Veterinary Section A.V.C. 16 Division		
War Diary	Villers Faucon	01/02/1918	28/02/1918
War Diary	Tincourt	01/03/1918	27/03/1918
War Diary	Sheet 62.D. N 33.d.9.2.	28/03/1918	19/04/1918
War Diary	36A H22d. 4.2 St Martin (Aire)	20/04/1918	26/04/1918

Type	Location	From	To
War Diary	St Martin (Aire)	27/04/1918	30/04/1918
War Diary	St Martin Aire 36a H.22.d.4.2	01/05/1918	10/05/1918
War Diary	St Martin Aire	11/05/1918	17/05/1918
War Diary	Wierre Au Bois Sheet 13-5d 2.8.	18/05/1918	31/05/1918
War Diary	Wierre Au Bois Calais 13	01/06/1918	21/06/1918
War Diary	Wierre Au Bois	22/06/1918	30/06/1918
War Diary	Wierre Au Bois (Calais 13.5D-2.2	01/07/1918	17/07/1918
War Diary	Wierre Au Bois	18/07/1918	31/07/1918
War Diary	Wierre Au. Bois Sheet 13 5.D.	01/08/1918	18/08/1918
War Diary	Wierre Au. Bois	19/08/1918	22/08/1918
War Diary	Barlin 44b K32 B 3.8	23/08/1918	31/08/1918
War Diary	Barlin. Sheet 44B K32.B. 3.8	01/09/1918	11/09/1918
War Diary	Barlin	12/09/1918	23/09/1918
War Diary	Drouvin K4.C.5.7.	24/09/1918	15/10/1918
War Diary	Annequin	16/10/1918	17/10/1918
War Diary	Bercleau	18/10/1918	18/10/1918
War Diary	Phalempin	19/10/1918	19/10/1918
War Diary	Templeuve	20/10/1918	22/10/1918
War Diary	La. Posterie Sheet 44 A5.d.86	23/10/1918	12/11/1918
War Diary	Rumes T.29.C.2.4 Sheet.37	13/11/1918	15/11/1918
War Diary	Enhevelin F.8.a.9.9. Sheet 44.a.	16/11/1918	30/11/1918
War Diary	Canchompre 2 F21.a 4.2 Sheet 44a.	01/12/1918	09/12/1918
War Diary	F21.a.4.2. Sheet 44.a.	11/12/1918	31/12/1918
War Diary	Ferme De Canchomprez F.21.a.4.2 Sheet 44.a	01/01/1919	28/02/1919
War Diary	Ferme De Canchomprez Templeare (Nord)	01/03/1919	31/03/1919
Heading	A April 1919 Missing		
War Diary	St Saulve Valencienines.	01/05/1919	11/07/1919
War Diary	Caserne Busutt Liouan	12/07/1919	31/07/1919
Heading	B Aug 1919 Missing		
War Diary	Douai.	01/09/1919	30/09/1919
Heading	C Sept 1919 Duplicated		
War Diary	Douai.	01/09/1919	30/09/1919
Miscellaneous	No. 1 District No. 12 Q.	11/11/1919	11/11/1919
Miscellaneous	D.A.Q.M.G. H.Q. No District	08/11/1919	08/11/1919
Miscellaneous	Veterinary No.1 District And Including 47th Mobile Veterinary Section		
Miscellaneous	Officer I/e R.A.V.C. Records Woolwich London S.E.	03/12/1919	03/12/1919
Miscellaneous	Veterinary No.1 District 47th Mobile Veterinary Section	21/04/1919	21/04/1919
Miscellaneous	Veterinary No.1 District including 47 Mobile Veterinary Section		
Miscellaneous	Herewith Intelligence Summary Veterinary No 1	25/11/1917	25/11/1917
Miscellaneous	Veterinary No.1 District 47 While Veterinary Sections	25/11/1919	25/11/1919

WO 95/1968/3

16 DIVN
DIVNL TROOPS
47th MOBILE VET. SECTION
1915 DEC – 1919 NOV

16TH DIVISION

47TH MOB. VETY SECTION
DEC 1915 - NOV 1919

47th Div: Feb; Weeks
Tot: I
15th–31st Dec
15/15
Jan '16.

36th Div

Dec '15
Nov '19

Army Form C. 2118.

WAR DIARY
or
INTELLIGENCE SUMMARY. 47th Mobile Veterinary Section

(Erase heading not required.)

Place	Date	Hour	Summary of Events and Information	Remarks and references to Appendices
Arrived Havre	19/12/15	9.0 a.m.	Entrained Havre Station 9 p.m.	
Arrived Rouquerel	20/12/15	8.30 p.m.	Travelled by road to Drouvain. Camped here until 24/12/15. No sick horses received.	
Arrived Gorny	24/12/15	1.30 p.m.	1 Horse admitted from 16th Train. 25/12/15 1 " " " " 7 R.J.R. 29/12/15 2 " " " " 16th Train " " 1 " " " " 16th D. Signal R.E. 30/12/15	1 Horse at 9th Munsters 29/12/15 " " H.Q. 16th Div " " This Horse not evacuated.
		(1/1/16)	1 Horse transferred to 5 R.V. Hospital at Will 31/12/15. Section H.Q. Gorny 1/1/16.	
Arrived Auchy au Bois	1/1/16	5.30 p.m.	1 Horse ad. from 1st E.A. R.S.A. Am. Col. 1/1/16 1 " " " " 16th Div. Sig. Co. R.E.) 1/1/16 (Evacuated on 1/1/16.)	1 Horse ad. from 3rd C.A.B. R.F.A. 1/1/16
Auchy au Bois	2/1/16		1 Horse ad. from M.M.P. } Not Evacuated 2/1/16 1 " " (L.D.) Ox Hus. 2nd Cav Bde 2/1/16 4th Bde.	1 Horse ad. from 7th Leinsters 2/1/16 47th Bde

W. Fenton Leird. M.R.C.V.S.
O.C. 47th M.V.S.

Army Form C. 2118.

WAR DIARY
or
INTELLIGENCE SUMMARY.

(Erase heading not required.)

47th Mobile Vet Section
No. 2

Instructions regarding War Diaries and Intelligence Summaries are contained in F. S. Regs., Part II. and the Staff Manual respectively. Title pages will be prepared in manuscript.

Place	Date	Hour	Summary of Events and Information	Remarks and references to Appendices
Auchy au Bois.	5/1/16		1 Horse L.D. collected from AMES. {These horses collected from AMES.	
			1 " A.D. " 1st E.a. R.F.A. { 3 Horses L.D. ad from E.a.S. R.F.A.	95 Horses + Mules Evacuated on the 7/1/16
			1 " " 3rd Essex (LIERRETT) " No. 10° Mac.Siv Train H.D.	
			5 " " 1/3 Lon Bde R.F.A. " 4th Bde R.H.A.	
			2 " " 1st Lon Bde R.F.A. 2 " " 1/2 Lon Bde R.F.A.	
			2 " " 1/2 5th L.B. R.F.A. 1 " L.D.	
			2 " " 5th E.a. R.a.C. 3rd E.a.B. R.F.A.	
				5 " E.a. R.a.C.
			5 Mules " " "	15 14 No V.H.
Auchy au Bois.	6/1/16		1 mule ad from 1/1 Lon. Bde. R.F.A. 2 Horses ad from 1/1 Lon Bde R.F.A.	Sgt Morgan
			2 Horses " 1st Essex Batt R.F.A. 4 " " 2 E.a.	L/Cpl Hopkins
			7 " " 3rd " " 9 " " 2nd Essex Batt R.F.A.	15 men
			1 " " 16th Div Sig Co 1 " " 9th Munsters	All well
			9 " " 1/5 Norfolk R.1st E.a R.F.A. 12 " " 2nd Norfolk R.1st E.a R.F.A.	7/1/16
			5 " " 3rd " " 18 " " Pak Am Col 1st E.a R.F.A.	
			3 " " 4th Bde R.H.a. 1 " " 1/2 London R R.F.A.	
				12 Evacuated on 7/1/1916
				1 Broke leg during entraining. went to Butcher

W. Winter Lieut R.A.V.C.
O.C. 47 Mvs

2353 Wt. W2544/1454 700,000 5/15 D.D.&L.   A.D.S.S./Forms/C 2118.

WAR DIARY
or
INTELLIGENCE SUMMARY.

Army Form C. 2118.

47th Mobile Vety Section

Place	Date	Hour	Summary of Events and Information	Remarks and references to Appendices
Auchy au Bois	7/1/16		8. Horses from 4th C.A. Bde R.F.A. / 1 " " H.Q. 45th In. Bde / 2. " " 3rd C.A.F.A. Bde. / 1 Horse ad from 1st R.L. Regt / 1 " " 4FB de Am Col 15th Div / 2 " " 2nd Div 32 G.Co.	28 Evacuated on 7/1/16 / 1 N.C.O / 3 Men / 15 M.V.S. / to Abbeville
"				
Auchy au Bois	8/1/16		3 Horses from 2nd C.A. F.A. Bde.	3 Horses from C.13 att R.H.A.
Auchy au Bois	9/1/16		1 Horse + 1 Mule from 54th C.U. D.A.C. / 21 " " 1/4th C.A. G.F.A.	1 HD Horse from 4 Remoloin
Auchy au Bois	10/1/16		1 Horse from 54th C.A. D.A.C. / 3 " " 3rd Norfolk B. E.A. / 3 " " Bde Am Col Ex / 1 " " Field Ambulance / 1 Collected from St HILAIRE COTTES (PSAP)	2 Horses from 1st Norfolk RFA EA / 7 " " 2nd " " / 1 " " Field Ambulance / 1 " " Norfolk RFA QFA Returned
Auchy au Bois	11/1/16		1 Horse Collected from Rely. / belonging to 433 C.M.R. J.A.S.C.	1 Horse + 9 Men RFA attached for duty / 5 Men from 10th D.A.C. / 1 NCO 4 Men from 3rd London Bde R.F.A.(T)

W Kerim Lieut Acc. OC 47th MVS.

Army Form C. 2118.

WAR DIARY
or
INTELLIGENCE SUMMARY.
(Erase heading not required.)

47th Mobile V.S. Section

Place	Date	Hour	Summary of Events and Information	Remarks and references to Appendices
Auchy au Bois	12/1/16		1 Horse collected from Esquedecques (sm) belonging to 1/1st London Bde R.F.A. 10 Horses from 1st London Bde R.F.A. 1 Mule from 16th Div Sig Co.	3 Horses collected from Fauquemberghes (4m) belonging to 1/2 Bom "Ben" Bt R.F.A T.F. 1 Horse from 16th Div Sig Co 2 Horses from 1/3rd Essex Batt. 4th C.L.Bde.	42 Horses Evacuated Cpl Taylor & men to Abbeville
Auchy au Bois	13/1/16		3 Horses from 3rd E.A. F.A. Bde	1 Horse from 7th Leicesters	
Auchy au Bois	14/1/16		1 Horse from 4th E.A. Ja Bde A.C. Headqtrs 16th Div. Don't Limit Jd. 1 " 2 "	1 Horse from 1st & 2nd Bde Cie 1 " " 14 S.C.° A.O.C.	Cpl Taylor & 5 men returned from Abbeville
Auchy au Bois	15/1/16		1 Horse from 2 E.A. Ja Bde 1 Mule from " 1 Horse from 112th Field Ambulance transferred to 3rd London R.F.A. 19/1/16	3 Horses from 3rd section 10th Div A.C.	16 Horses Evacuated Cpl Smyth & Man to Abbeville

W Newton Lieut AVC
Oc 47 M.V.S.

Army Form C. 2118

WAR DIARY
or
INTELLIGENCE SUMMARY.
(Erase heading not required.)

H.Q. Mobile Vet Section

Place	Date	Hour	Summary of Events and Information	Remarks and references to Appendices
Aucky au Bois	16/1/16		7 mules from 54th E.A. F.A.C. 24 Horses from 54th E.A. F.A.C. 3 Horses from 4 E.A. R.F.A. 13th The shippen to H.Qs.	
Aucky au Bois	17/1/16		3 Horses from 3rd E.A. L.A. Bde. 3 " " 1/1 E.A. Bde R.F.A. 2 " " 54 Sardar 1 mule " " 3 Horses from 2nd E. A.L.A. Bat. 8th V. Battle.	Cpt. Godfrey 1 mule returned from Abbeville. 1st Maryor given to horses to Abbeville
Aucky au Bois	18/1/16		1 Horse from 16 Div Train 142 A.S.C.	
Aucky au Bois	19/1/16		1 Horse from 2nd Herts Batt. 4th E.A. R.A.	Sgt Manger 5th Hampshire Abbeville 19/1/15 G.S.W. min to W.S.
Aucky au Bois	20/1/16		6 Horses from 1/3 London Bde R.A. 1 " " 1st E.A. R.A. 1 " " 16th Div Am Col 3 Section.	1 Horse from 48th Inf Bde. 1 mule " 48th Inf Bde

W. Robin Luis R.V.C.
OC. H.Q. MVS

Army Form C. 2118.

WAR DIARY
or
INTELLIGENCE SUMMARY.

(Erase heading not required.)

47th Mobile Vet Section

Place	Date	Hour	Summary of Events and Information	Remarks and references to Appendices
Auchy au Bois	21/1/16		2 Horses from Remount Depot.	
Auchy au Bois	22/1/16		9 Horses from 1/3 Lon Bde RFA	
Auchy au Bois	23/1/16		1 Horse from 112th Field Ambulance 1 " Transferred O.C. R from 47th Mobile V. Sec.	1 Horse from 54th S.A.R.A.C.	Pte Finlayson returning from 42 by Res 23/1/16
Auchy au Bois	24/1/16		3 Horses from 1/3 Lon Bde RFA	Pte Shepherd returning from Headquarters
Auchy au Bois	25/1/16		1 Horse from 9 Batt R Munster Fus. 6 " " 2nd Aug L.A. Bde 4 " " 4 " " " "	2 Mules from 35th T.M.B 1 Horse " 1/3 Lon Bde RFA 3 " " 3rd S.A.F.A. Bde	Cpl Winckly 4 Men & 35th Horses to Lillers 24/1/15
Auchy au Bois	26/1/16		1 Mule from Collecting Stn "Allouay" Unit unknown 2 Horses from 3rd S.A. L.A. Bde	1 Horse from 54th S.A. F.A. 3 " " 4 S.A. F.A. 3 " " 33 D.A.C. 3 Res.	Lt Curtis Rollins 1st Aumont 4/Port New Horse 3/1/16

Anton L. M.E
D.C. Ly 47 M.V.S

Army Form C. 2118

WAR DIARY
or
INTELLIGENCE SUMMARY.
(Erase heading not required.)

47th Mobile Vet Section

Place	Date	Hour	Summary of Events and Information	Remarks and references to Appendices
Auchy au Bois	27/1/16		1 Horse from 1/3 Bde R.F.A. 2 Horses from 1/6 Bde R.F.A. " " 1st Royal Irish Rifles 1 Mule from 7th Royal Irish Rifles " " Collector for Reserve First Unknown	Capt Maitland & 4 men returned from Abbeville
Auchy au Bois	28/1/16		1 Horse from 1st K. Bde R.F.A. 1 Horse from 9th Dublins	
Auchy au Bois	29/1/16		1 Horse from 16th Div Div Coy	Cpl Taylor & 4 Men and 28 Horses to Abbeville
Auchy au Bois	30/1/16			
Auchy au Bois	31/1/16		1 Horse from 5th Royal Dublin Fus. 3 Horses from 1st East Ang Bde R.F.A. 1 Mule " 1st East Ang Bde R.F.A. Collector at Esquin	Cpl Taylor & Men from Abbeville

W. Winton Lund A.V.C.
O.C. 47th M.V.S.

47th Moh: Vet: Sect:
16   Vol: 2

Army Form C. 2118.

"47th Mobilisation A.V.C." 16th Division

WAR DIARY
or
INTELLIGENCE SUMMARY.
(Erase heading not required.)

February 1916

Place	Date	Hour	Summary of Events and Information	Remarks and references to Appendices
Auchy aux Bois	1/2/1916	8.0 a.m	Cpl Taylor & driver & Rennety & driver to Cpl Dur of 1/2 London Mobile with Schinker, en route to Attenville by road. To exchange 5.8 hander for Blunt Horse Ambulance. 1 Horse C/3 807 Dockinger & Baines (Glanders case) shot. 2nd Anglian Base R.S.R. 1 Horse Destroyed.	
	2/2/16	8.0 am	Cpl Godfrey, Driver + 3 Pts to Rebecque to collect 6 Horses 4 mule on compliance with orders from DDVS. belonging to Unit 1/1st London Base R.S.A.	
		8.30 am	Lieut Renton + Pte Chappell to C/o R8. Millieres 73 animals, went forward and collected one horse from M. Salinque (Francois) at Ames (Animals 23 Animals) 6340 Sgt Wilshaw arrived from 175th Fld Ros R.S.A. 34th Division	
	3/2/16	8.30 am	Lt Renton + Pte Chappell to C/o R8's & Sdhgr. to Mallein 36 animals. 6340 Sgt Wilshaw to 47. Inf'y Bde Hdqrs in place of Pte Shells. Khaki Boot, Rifle Inspection by Lt Renton Seven animals' names to Isolation Officer 48th Inf'y Bde (2 mules Animitis)	
	4/2/16	9.30 am	Two horses brought from Div. & Hqrs. to be Malleined	
	5/2/16	9.0 am	Lt Renton + Pte Chappell to RSs to Mallein 18 animals. Evacuates 21 animals to Attenville. Cpl Eastry Ψ/o a/Cpl & Sheens + Pte Shells after delivery of animals Pte Shells left for R/3 Hospital Boulogne a/Cpl Hopwin Ψ/o (1 Horse Animitis)	
	6/2/16	9.0 am	Pte Palmer collected horse from Return Depot (Anuck) 6th R Irish Regt. 2 mules from RSs to be delivered by Wilshelm Lt Renton + 2 Ptes to Witterness to collect three animals, only one mule be brought in on account of large sums due for keep of animals owing to them formed left 3/5 of inhabitants Lt Renton obtained A.D.V.S. on matter. Cpl Miller off 1/2 London Mobile arrived with float on return from Attenville (2 Horses) off 1/2 London Mobile left for Attack by Unit	
	7/2/16	8.0 am	C/3 368 1 Horse died, Post mortem 2pm, then buried according to regulation	

Army Form C. 2118.

WAR DIARY
or
INTELLIGENCE SUMMARY.

47th Mobile Section AVC
16th Division
February 1916. Contd.

(Erase heading not required.)

Instructions regarding War Diaries and Intelligence Summaries are contained in F.S. Regs., Part II. and the Staff Manual respectively. Title pages will be prepared in manuscript.

Place	Date	Hour	Summary of Events and Information	Remarks and references to Appendices
Montigny aux Bois	8/2/16	9.0 am	Cpl Godfrey returned from Abbeville reported a/Cpl Hopkins & the sick duty left for Boulogne 6/2/16 2 pm	
		1 pm	a/Cpl Hopkins returned from Boulogne reports the duty carried out	
		2 pm	Cpl Taylor +2 Privates with Float to collect horse Unit 8th R Dublin Fus.	
		3.30 pm	Lieut Renton & Pte Quinn to Wierre-Effroy collected horse from inhabitant (6 Animals admitted)	
	9/2/16		Horse C/3372 B.om. Army 2 Animals admitted	
	10/2/16	2.0 am	1 Horse C/3372 Died of Tetanus was buried 10 am Stalls thoroughly cleaned & disinfected.	
		9.0 am	Collected from Paddock all horses ready for evacuation	
		2 pm	Lieut Renton & Private to Wittemesse checked last of the three animals which has been left with inhabitants. (2 Animals admitted)	
	11/2/16	7.30 am	Float to railhead with horse for evacuation	
		11.0 am	Evacuated 23 Animals to Base, another first case taken with same. (Admitted 7 Animals)	
			Cpl Taylor met 3 men S/O	
	12/2/16		Commenced visiting new shed for sick animals	
	13/2/16	9 am	Float taken to Febvin Palfart to collect one Horse C/3 390 Unit Hqrs 47 Infty Bde. (2 animals admitted)	
	14/2/16	9.15 am	Cpl Taylor & party from Abbeville duty carried out, now sick animals	
		12 am	1 Horse evacuated to Base. (2/flat case) a/Cpl Hopkins S/o.	
		5 pm	Cpl Strickland Driver with 6/5 Limber & mules arrived in coup to attend by Road up to DHS	
		7.30 pm	Lieut Renton Pte Ross to Wierre-Effroy to attend wounded (French) horse injured by motor lorry (2 animals admitted)	
	15/2/16	8.30 am	Cpl Strickland & party continued journey	
		10.30 am	Inspection by H.R.H. Prince Arthur of Connaught, D.D.V.S. in attendance	
		3 pm	Lt Renton to Wicheken to attend wounded (French) Horse	
	16/2/16	9 am	Pte Quinn to railhead with saddle horse to meet a/Cpl Hopkins returned from Abbeville Repaired sheds of the gale. (2 Animals admitted)	

WAR DIARY or INTELLIGENCE SUMMARY.

Army Form C. 2118.

47th Mobile Section A.V.C.
16th Division

February Column

Place	Date	Hour	Summary of Events and Information	Remarks and references to Appendices
Authy au Bois	17/2/16	11 am	Evacuated 7 horses to Abbeville. Cpl Soapey S/C. Thoroughbreds. Overshoes collected in flight from 48th Div Tpt & Arm Hqrs.	(3 Horses Admitted)
	18/2/16	9 am	Lt Lenton to Wisterham to attend General Horse Shed repairs completed. Orders to make Regl Arm also Sufficient in no Sufficient quantities to supply divisional units, noted local units, those for show wounds.	(admitted)
	19/2/16	7.30 am	Horse taken to Ames to collect horse suffering from Johnin (chipped Wound) Unit 8th Munster	
		9 am	Pte Row to Westerham for dressing of french horse. Pte Scott with saddle horse to railhead to meet Cpl Soapey returning from Abbeville.	(5 Animals Admitted)
	20/2/16	9 am	Lieut Lenton Buchanan all section horses + two Indian horses (cycleators) Sgt. 26 animals Corps rations to hand. Sgt Wayman promoted to rank of Staff Sergeant from Feb 18th/16 Cpl Strickland Driver Left returning from Abbeville Stables Discharged for 1 S/S horses CP3. 39. Cured. Issued to T.O. 48th D/y Tpt Pte.	(4 Animals Admitted)
		5 pm		
	21/2/16	8.30 am	Cpl Strickland left with Dvr + Stout 18 horses and 4/9th W.I.T.	
		8 am	Lieut Lenton Cpl Taylor + 3 Privates to Mametz to collect horses 47 Horse Unit 35th DAC	
		1.30 pm	o/c Cpl Hopkins with horse to Mametz to collect horse found to be unfit to travel	
		4 pm	Lieut Lenton to Ayres 48th Divl Rlde. Horseshoers gave lecture on "Fees Feeding" (horse) to General Perrier, Staff, O/C Supplies & Transport Officers.	(15 Animals Admitted)
	22/2/16	6.30 am	Staff Sgt Wayman to Ames to arrange with VO O/c 1/3 London Bus to send 7 of the 14 Docks Animals the admitted. To railhead ready to join our shipment at 11 am.	
		9 am	S.S Wayman back to make another journey to Ames to superintend the arrangement.	
		11 am	Evacuated 34 Animals (West-Jais) 1 Cpl Taylor 2 Drs D/c Jones as witness by party with those evacuated 7 Animals, mainly softed invaccuation ill.	(21 Animals Admitted)
		4 pm	Horse journed to 10th DAC	
	23/2/16	10 am	Lieut Lenton to Pezy-adieque ballooning with 8DVS returned 3 pm. Staff Sgt Wayman to Warle Stern to Mels Stone Stone. Nd for Lieut Stone. Evacuated one ill horse. (wind sucker)	(6 Animals Admitted)

Army Form C. 2118.

47th Mobile Section MVC
16th Division
February 1916 (Continued)

WAR DIARY
or
INTELLIGENCE SUMMARY.
(Erase heading not required.)

Place	Date	Hour	Summary of Events and Information	Remarks and references to Appendices
Authy-aux-Bois	24/2/16	11 am	Evacuated 31 Animals. Cpl Godfrey i/c. Two of these were collected from Lieges & taken straight to railhead. Cpl Taylor & party arrived from Attilloue	(1 Animal Evacuated)
	25/2/16	10 am	Lt Kenton to Beyencourt to inspect animals reported on the 23rd (ADVS enquires)	
		6.30 pm	Cpl Taylor & 2 men took horse float to collect horse too lame to walk, left on road through Bayeux Blangie	
		7.45 pm	Lt Kenton left to join the above party, could not find sick horse, roads very bad to return (snow)	(1 Animal Admitted)
	26/2/16	11 am	Staff Sgt Wignan with Sheeny Smith left to meet party with float, returned 12.30 with two. They were on their way back, bringing another sick animal collected at Wittornesse, whole party returned by 3 pm. (N345) Horse died on journey (3 Animals Admitted)	
	27/2/16	8.30 am	Cpl Godfrey & party returned from Attilloue	
		11 am	Evacuated 26 Animals. Sgt Wignan & 3 men i/c.	
			Remainder Shoes & packed up all time ready to move under orders	
	8.30 pm		Message not to move until further orders.	
	9 pm		Lt Kenton to S.S.O. to arrange for Rations & forage. Reply there at 9 am 28th.	
	28/2/16	7 am	Cpl Colman to Reuver (near Area) with correspondence	
		9 am	Lieut Kenton with party (float) to St Quentin for horse, on arrival found to be dead.	
			Brought on another sick horse from same village	
		8.30 am	Orderly Person i/c Kit baggage Wagon & Pair, reported ready for move	
		4 pm	Lt Kenton to I Battery RHA, on receipt of message re Animal not found in the dist, by Gillain followed by float to join them.	
	29/2/16	9.30 am	Lt Murphy an Officer for Kendrew (in Reserve) by next arrived about 2.45 pm.	(1 Animal Admitted)
		4 pm	Cpl Burges & party returned from Attilloue	

Lt Col, R.A.M.C.
A.D.V.S.

47 M. v. Seek
Vol 3

Army Form C. 2118.

No. 1.

WAR DIARY

INTELLIGENCE SUMMARY.

(Erase heading not required.)

March 1916

47th Mobile Section AVC

Instructions regarding War Diaries and Intelligence Summaries are contained in F. S. Regs., Part II. and the Staff Manual respectively. Title pages will be prepared in manuscript.

Place	Date	Hour	Summary of Events and Information	Remarks and references to Appendices
LA PERRIERE BUSNES	1/3/16	10.a.m	Pte Palmer with ration for fatigue party left behind at Auchy auBois, three to 1/Kings with ASC T.S. (Co Car) to collect horse, unit, 18.0 Killer Rota, not completed	
		12.30pm	Sgt Morgan + 3 men returned from Athille on completion of evacuation duty	
		"	S/S. 10729 Sgt David W. arrived for duty from No 19. Vety Hospital	
		4pm	Float for three left S/o 9 am R.E.S 1/R Irish Inish at Bruneltes, Buy to various directions horse could not be located, 7pm message with free direction received. Pte Hopkins sent for food, horse watered & fed.	(One animal admitted)
	2/3/16	8.0 am	Float to Bruneltes for horse CB 499, taken temp. to 1/2 London Mobile Killen, ready for evacuation	
		9.0 am	Lt Hinton to Auchy au Bois to attend sick animals left behind	
			Pte Florence to 157th & Fe R.E clipped unruled limbers	
			Limber to Auchy auBois for dead cover limber	(10 animals admitted)
		10.0 am	Staff Sgt Wickham departed to take up duty at R.O.S Veterinary Hospital	
	3/3/16	8 am	Float to Auchy au Bois made two journeys to take two animals to 1/2 London Mobile Sec Vy Hosp, ready for evacuation	
		9 am	Pte Burleigh & 47th Sgt Bale sent on duty to Messines in place of A.V.C Sgt granick	
			Lt Canton to inspect animals of 157 Br. Sirta Co R.E Bi. (Co V.O S/C)	
		2 pm	Cpl Scraggy + 3 men (fatigue party) returned from Auchy au Bois	
			Evacuated 6 animals to Base A Veterinary S/O. CB4493. Horse Destroyed this Sgnd Lut Wilson US. Inp Sect	(13 animals admitted)
	4/3/16	9 am	Float to Bruneu to collect CB 527. 7th Royal Irish Rifles	
			Evacuated 22 animals to Base a/Cpl Ross & 2 men S/C	(admitted 30 animals)
	5/3/16	3.0 pm	Pte Palmer to Auchy au Bois on 15mi arranged deposal of CB 5493 Horse destroyed (admitted admiralty)	
	6/3/16	7.0 am	Float to Bourecq collected mule CB 5357 157th Co R.E taken straight to Railway ready for evacuation	
		8.30am	a/Cpl Savage returned from Base. 8pm Evacuated 21 animals Cpl Sayler + 2 men S/C	
		2.30pm	Lt Pitt Kin W W58A/1/14100,000 6/14 D.D.&L Veterinary Senior	(10 animals admitted)

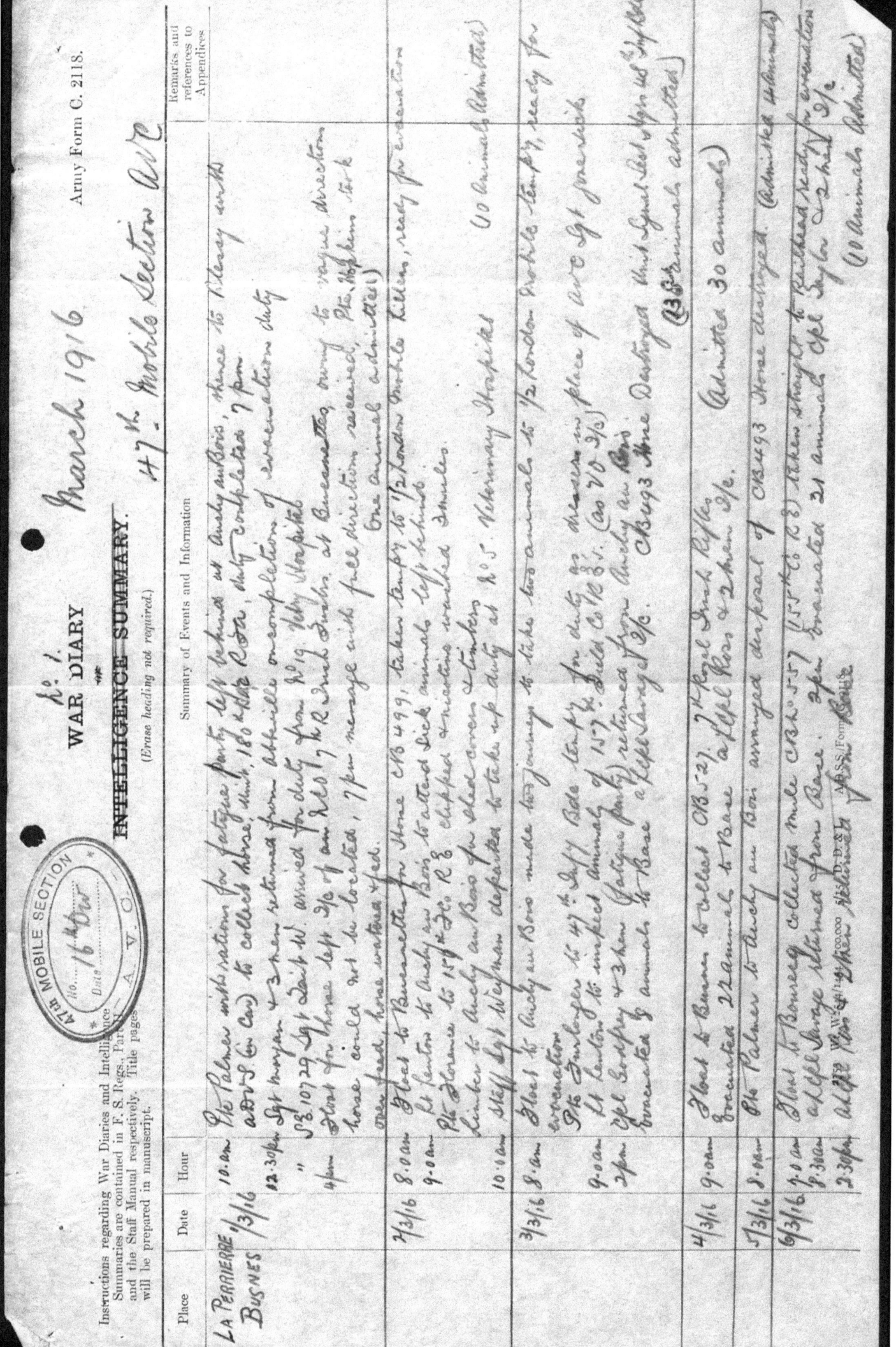

Army Form C. 2118.

WAR DIARY
INTELLIGENCE SUMMARY
(Erase heading not required.)

March 1916.

No. 2

4) Mobile Section AVC

Instructions regarding War Diaries and Intelligence Summaries are contained in F.S. Regs., Part II. and the Staff Manual respectively. Title pages will be prepared in manuscript.

Place	Date	Hour	Summary of Events and Information	Remarks and references to Appendices
LA PERRIERRE BUSNES	7/3/16		2 animals admitted	
	8/3/16	7.30am	Went to Bruaysto for horse CB S72. 180th Bde RFA taken to railhead ready for evacuation	
		2pm	Evacuated 16 animals (Plcataous) ACPL Savage 4 Jan 36.	
		3.30pm	Went to Ham en Artois for horse CB 574 7th R. Irish Rifles	
			(3 animals admitted)	
	9/3/16	6.0am	Packing & preparing for move.	
		1.0pm	Left for new area. Billets originally occupied by 12th London Battn in Rue De Perrier	
			arrived new billet about 3pm. Sent supplies returned to La Perriere for lame horse & another	
			load. CB S71. Died Horse 177 RHA RSA.	
			(Admitted 5 animals)	
LILLERS	10/3/16	7.0am	Went & Mule started for making of two tips to La Perriere for two lame horse and	
			two lock Italian sheet irons timber Etc (4 animals admitted) 1 flat back	
			ACPL Savage man returned from base 3 collected from inhabitants at	
		2pm	Inspection by D.D.V.S. D.D.V.S. & A.D.V.S.	
		3pm	A.D.V.S. Operations on French Army Horse. LA MICQUELLERIE - CHATEAUCOTES 4 ISBERGUE	
	11/3/16	9am	Went to Ecleme for horse CB S75. Fatigue Party returned from La Perriere	
		2pm	Evacuated 7 animals ACPL Savage 3/c.	
	12/3/16	9.0am	Mule CB S90 Collected Meat (15th Dragtly G) (6 animals admitted)	
			Mule CB S91. Collected from Doham Lt Lenton & Pte Palmer	
		6pm	Man with sick horse of 77 2 Field Ambulance 2.5m. Div en route to Bruay stayed overnight	
		8.30pm	Sgt Goodley 2383 AVC reported from 160th Bde RSA. Taken on Strength temp for duty	
	13/3/16		4 animals admitted	
			All mobilization table stores sorted out & that taken off other stores surplus owing to difficulty of	
			transport when moving into new areas.	

Army Form C. 2118.

WAR DIARY No 3. March 1916

INTELLIGENCE SUMMARY.

(Erase heading not required.)

47 Mobile Veter. A/C

Place	Date	Hour	Summary of Events and Information	Remarks and references to Appendices
LILLERS	14/3/16	10.30	Lt Lenton to Railhead to inspect remounts. A/Cpl Savage returned from Base. Evacuated 15 animals A/Cpl Hopkins & Pte Wilkes I/c.	(Animals Admitted)
		2pm	7 animals Admitted	
	15/3/16		CB 16 Collected males lectures	
	16/3/16	1pm	Evacuated 13 animals A/Cpl Savage & 1 man I/c. 3 animals Admitted	
	17/3/16		A/Cpl Hopkins Pte Wilkes returned from Bac Hoepl. Admitted 9 animals	
	18/3/16		CB 31. Horse collected float 177th Sec RFA Evacuated 22 animals to Base Hospital No.13. A/Cpl Chester A/Cpl Blackburn & 2 men I/c. Admitted 22 animals.	
	19/3/16	10-30am	Pte Campbell 397) Transport driver 18 Hordon Regt 47th Div left by train for Journey Therbonne Pte came here on the 17 inst with Lance Corde came from Ambulance here before Blandele that worked from 7am to 5pm his horses wer admitted some 33 kilos from here. the horse was found to be too lame we admitted for evacuation (Admitted 7 animals)	
		1pm	Evacuated 15 animals A/Cpl Chester & 1 man I/c.	(Animals Admitted)
	20/3/16		Collected in float 1 Horse CB 58 182 Bge RFA, 1 Horse CB 58 177 Bde RFA Lt Lenton inspected 120 remounts at Railhead, 20 of which were admitted Sick. A/Cpl Savage 4 men returned. A/Cpl Blackburn 2 men returned.	(8 animals Admitted)
		1pm		
	21/3/16		A/Cpl Ross returned. Evacuated 7 animals A/Cpl Stephenson I/c.	(Admitted 5 animals 1 foot case)
	22/3/16		Collected 2 horses from Inhabitants at Bergette & 1 males Coll 1 foot case from 169AC.	(7 animals Admitted)
	23/3/16		A/Cpl Hopkins returned from Beuf CA Ed. 1 foot case from Han. En-Artois.	
	24/3/16		2383 Pt Snaddey J. Transferred for duty with D-65 177th Sec VSR.	8 animals Admitted 1 foot case
	25/3/16		Evacuated 21 animals A/Cpl Savage & 1 man I/c. 6 men arrived from divisional company for fatigue purposes	5 animals Admitted (3 collected from Railway)

Army Form C. 2118.

WAR DIARY No 4
INTELLIGENCE SUMMARY
#7 Mobile Section A.V.C.
March 1916

(Erase heading not required.)

Place	Date	Hour	Summary of Events and Information	Remarks and references to Appendices
LILLERS	26/3/16	10am	Cpl Taylor & Pte Rose advance party to new area (27th Mobile)	
		11am	L/Cpl Miller & Pte Turner arrived advance party of 27th M.V.S. to take over details	
		2pm	Pte Wiltshaw 6340 arrived #7 attached handed over to Camp commandant 29th 7.0 am returned to #7 M.V.S. on arrival, any new over evening of 27th. Horse collected Pte 177 transferred 17A. (Animals admitted) transferred 7 animals #Cpl Spires O/C	
	27/3/16		Left Lillers at 10 am for new area arrived about 3 pm NOEUX LES MINES handed over to 27th M.V.S. C/B.5.27. 5.0 h/pwr from Army C/B.100 4101. Pte Barlinger returned for duty from #7 Empty stable. Pte Wiltshaw 6340 Pte C. Sent #7 attached	
		6pm	#Cpl Spires returned. Station to be drawn at K. head stores Rations	(received supplemental)
NOEUX LES MINES 28/3/16				(Animals (different))
	29/3/16		1 animal admitted. Erected shed for isolation cases.	
	30/3/16		Admitted 8 animals. 1 Collected pool from 12 D.A.C. Levelled approach & dug all starting	
			motor shed for cookhouse	
	31/3/16		3.02794 Dvn Hayworth 15A Admitted ad & Driver departed on leave Act 31st to April 7/16. Evacuated 7 animals #Cpl Barlinger O/c Built new latrine. Latrines up all stations, sheds, standings ready for covering all over with slag	

Wenton Sims M.C.
O.C. 47" M.V.S.

XVI Divion.

WAR DIARY or **INTELLIGENCE SUMMARY.** 471st Mobile Section A.V.C.

Army Form C. 2118.

Vol 43
April

Place	Date	Hour	Summary of Events and Information	Remarks and references to Appendices
Nouveau Leo Quinn	Apl 1/16	8 am	6 Privates sent to or attached to 16th Divisional Train Coy	(2 animals admitted)
	Apl 2	9 am	C.B. 128 Collected in float A/Cpl Savage returned from tent A del Grace in float Thurs Thurs	(9 animals admitted)
	Apl 3		Evacuated 21 animals A/Cpl Savage + 2 men S/C	(Admitted 3 animals) 1 fine care
	" 4th	2.30 am	Message from A.D.V.S. to collect in float Horse supposed Hat kicked by Cpl Brady + 2 men with float. Animal found to be too bad for removal, destroyed	(Admitted 5 animals) (1 glanders C.ro.
	" 5th		St Rondre acting A.D.V.S. Accompanied on tour of Major Mackenzie A/Cpl Savage + 2 men returned	(Admitted 6 animals)
	6th		Evacuated 20 animals. A/Cpl Blackburn + 2 men S/C	
	7th		A/Cpl Savage + 2 men returned	(4 animals admitted)
	8th		Pte Maynard returned from leave (England) A/Cpl Blackburn + 2 men returned	Admitted 6 animals
	9th		Evacuated 8 animals A/Cpl Savage S/C. Admitted 2 animals from the outlying post	
	10th		Admitted 12 animals	
	11th		A/Cpl Savage returned Pte Godfrey + Pte Rees on leave to (England)	Admitted 7 animals
	12th	5.30 pm	Evacuated 21 animals A/Cpl Stephens + 2 men to C Squadron 1st King Edwards Horse (Brig. H.Q.) to Inspection of Army Horses (Brig H.Q.) Horse reported to be examined before being shipped home. 5 animals not passed and 1 admitted (1 animal)	
	13th	7.30 am	Cpl Savage finished town inspection. 9 horses killed on duty watering times (Elm R.) 111st Gul Arolan (Admitted 3 animals)	

Army Form C. 2118.

WAR DIARY
or
INTELLIGENCE SUMMARY.
(Erase heading not required.)

Army No 2 April

47th Mobile Section A/C

Instructions regarding War Diaries and Intelligence Summaries are contained in F.S. Regs., Part II. and the Staff Manual respectively. Title pages will be prepared in manuscript.

Place	Date	Hour	Summary of Events and Information	Remarks and references to Appendices
Troyes Bry hum	April 14th		Returned 20 tacks frokin to Ordnance Railhead in compliance with DRO	(9 Animals Admitted)
	15th		A.D.V.S. returned from leave. Took over from Lt Lenton. Pte Shepherd to Semp. derived to W.V.S.	6 Animals Admitted
	16th		Evacuated 16 animals a L/Cpl Palmer + 3 men S/c	(Admitted 12 animals)
	17th	6pm	Verification Pte Savage transferred to first anglophone Post Station Lt Lenton, Sgt Morgan, Dentryworth + Pte Blackburn to Philosophe with first pr C/3 281	(Admitted (12 animals)
		8pm	Cpl Godfrey returned from leave	
	18th		A/L/Cpl Parks + Barnes returned. Evacuated 9 animals. L/Cpl Hopkins S/c 5 remount 5 sent in by D.S.R units not separated at Bichuse as animal of same, ad cleaned by 5:30pm.	(Admitted 10 appendix)
	19th		Evacuated 40 animals Cpl Godfrey + 4 men S/c	(Admitted 3 9 Animals)
	20th		A/L/Cpl Hopkins returned. Horse belonging to Q.182 R/Sds C.S.R fallen by stars to V/S Front takes to convey animal to Buckelow.	(8 animals Admitted)
	21st		Cpl Seafry party returned. Pte Ren. returned from leave Sergts. +c Mt V.S. Front. Pte Hopkin per C/3 281	(12 Animals Admitted)
	22nd		C/3 281 (3 men) Died. G.V.S (Col Ligget) Sgt Morgan S/c to Pte Burns, B.C.E W Store. C/3 282 start repairs. Evacuated 10 horses + 1 bld. L/Cpl Bates + 2 men S/c 1027 S. Pte Shepherd to 111th Field Ambulance Admitted 12 men S/c knee strangment	(13 animals Admitted) Result of a kick by horse
	23rd		Evacuated 16 animals a L/Cpl Ron + Downes S/c. Verification from 111 Field Ambulance 1123 S. Pte Shipper returned to B'1 Casualty Clearing Station	(Admitted 9 animals)
	24th		A/L/Cpl Downes + 2 men returned	(Admitted 14 Animals)

Signed A.V.C.
W. D.V.S

Army Form C. 2118.

WAR DIARY
or
INTELLIGENCE SUMMARY.
(Erase heading not required.)

47th Mobile Section A.V.C.

Instructions regarding War Diaries and Intelligence Summaries are contained in F. S. Regs., Part II. and the Staff Manual respectively. Title pages will be prepared in manuscript.

Place	Date	Hour	Summary of Events and Information	Remarks and references to Appendices
Roeux les Mines (Mines)	April 25th		Evacuated 24 animals. A/Cpl Chappell J/C. with 2 men + Convoy returned. D.R.O. 0.522 Dated 20/4/16. States Lieut Fenton A.V.C. will give a course in ? Farriers on ? horse management to officers R&W men of 1st horse Transport of Brigade no reserve who desire to do so. (Admitted 25 animals.)	
	26th		C/13 316 Horse destroyed. Sent to Butcher. Lt Fenton lectured as above. (9 animals Admitted)	
	27th		A/Cpl Chappell + 2 men returned. Evacuated 32 animals. A/Cpl Denman + 3 men J/C. No lectures by Lieut Fenton Brigade moved to ? (Admitted 19 animals)	
	28th		Lieut Fenton attended sick cases of 1st horse Transport (France). No lecture Rate to attend to (Admitted 8 animals)	
	29th		Evacuated 14 animals. A/Cpl Roe + Palmer J/C. C/13 367 Destroyed sent to Butcher. A/Cpl Denman + 2 men returned. No lectures Brigade changed over. (Admitted 8 animals)	
	30th		Orders sent to transfer no 10729 Sgt Jack from 47th M.V.S to O/Sgt 60th Sec G.S.? 12 noon. Rifle inspection Horse Transfer carried out. (Admitted 2 animals)	

[Signature]
A.V.C.

[Signature]
O.C.

WAR DIARY or INTELLIGENCE SUMMARY

Army Form C. 2118.

47th Mobile Veterinary Section. A.V.C. 16th Divn.

Place	Date	Hour	Summary of Events and Information	Remarks and references to Appendices
NIEUX LES MINES	May 1/16		A/Cpl Ross & Pte Palmer returned from Base Vety Hospital on completion of convalescence of horses C/S 393 Q. 1 Horse collected Headquarters on M.V.S./ford. Wants Blankets. Horse Rugs etc returned to Ordnance (2 animals admitted)	
	May 2nd	9 am	Evacuated 8 animals a/Cpl Downs 9/c. 2 animals of 182nd Bde R.F.A. Destroyed. Sold to Butcher Lieut Lowton gone a lecture on Horse Arrangement 9/c to 47th & 9/c/17 Bde Somerford.	Admitted 5 animals
	May 3rd		Evacuated 8 animals a/Cpl Hopkin 9/c. Pte Squire granted leave to England May 4th to 6.11-	Admitted 9 animals
	4th		A/Cpl Downs returned. a/Cpl Ross 9/c. Limber sent to Hd/gruel 4 -collect two officers Vety chech for A.D.V.S. from 0/c 4th Reserve Park	Admitted 26 animals
	5th		Lieut Lowton granted leave to England May 5th to 1673rd Evacuated 28 animals a/Cpl Sent & Private Barnes & Palmer 9/c. C10.36, Mule destroyed sale to Butcher	3 animals admitted
	6th		a/Cpl Ross returned. Pte Luggs returned from 1st Corps rest Station CB41 & L2 attached. M.V.S./ford from Vandieucourt and Headgruvel	6 animals admitted
	7th		A/Cpl Sent 42 hour returned	2 cm animals admitted
	8th		CB 16 collected M.V.S./ford from Vardrieucourt	16 animals admitted
	9th		Evacuated 24 animals A/Cpl Blackburn Pte Case Barnes, Florence & Hopkyn 9/c.	1 animal admitted
	10th		4702 Pte Sriage admitted to Hospital	
	11th		A/Cpl Blackburn 24 hrs returned. CB74. 1 Horse collected M.V.S./ford from Philosophe	3 animals admitted
	12th		Pte Squire returned from leave delayed 24 hour at Boulogne. M.V.S./ford collected 1 Horse C/S 77 from Bully Grenay	4 animals admitted
	13th		Evacuated 36 animals a/Cpl Hopkins, Pte Chapel Downs, Cribbs, Florence 9/c. Notification from 0/c 111th Field Ambulance Pte Sriage evacuated by 1st M.A.C. dated 17/5/16	Admitted 24 animals /Private I died 11/5/15 fell at Port

Army Form C. 2118.

47th Mobile Veterinary Section AVC
1st Div
16th Div

WAR DIARY or INTELLIGENCE SUMMARY.
(Erase heading not required.)

Place	Date	Hour	Summary of Events and Information	Remarks and references to Appendices
NOEUX-LES-MINES	May 14th/16		Lieut Renton returned from leave	Animals 1
	15th		R/Cpl Hopkins to run returned. Lieut Renton Clerk to duty in ADVS's office in relief for clerk on leave	12
	16th		14193 Pte Knott J.W. arrived as reinforcement	3
	17th		Repatriated for 10275 Pte Shepherd. Animals NIL By land. Cpl Arnolds Godman Sgt Marsh Pte Barnes Jenner Stanley Forbridge Hopkins Palmer Stenning S/c Pte Ross & Dvr Kirby reported to O/C 16 MVS & are duly reported for services as consult of branch wireless	50
	18th		1793 Pte Anderson B AVC arrived from 27th/16 MV Sn as reinforcement Cpl Taylor granted leave to England 19th to 28th May	1
	19th			
	20th			6
	21st		14397 Sgt Fox AVC from 23rd Mobile 12th Div. 2nd Re Reinforcement to HQ 180 Rifle	16 (1 Sec)
	22nd		Dvr Ruby transferred to Army Signal School LISTRES, left 9am for 9 days leave approx. 2 days	
	23rd		Spr Cpl Godfrey 4/8 to sub din returned. KNJ685 Pte Lucas I AVC arrived from R.Q.J. Hospital as reinforcement	6
	24th		Dvr Hogarth Pte Scott on duty with horses. horse drillen accident in which a branch injured his upper eye land. Section inspected and present Cpl Godfrey 4/5 Nov.S/c	5
	25th		Spr Godfrey granted leave by 29th June 4th Lt to lines of 1st Mobile Veto S/c (Re Ross) assisted horses killed wounded evacuated to open R.R.	6
			Battalion 3 admitted to Mobile Section on evacuation, Open R magazeni Walland Evacuated horse	29
	26th		Cpl Godfrey Dvr Norr returned	10
	27th		Cpl Taylor returned from leave. CMS 2×4. 1 Horse Collection Point Pres Vinselins	3
	28th		Open Field Return Arrivals at Dargingtin or Dargingtin on horse management & Officers NCOs 6th Divt Artillery	
	29th		CMS 2×2 Dockyard veterinary 1 Horse 162nd Rosa Regt. 2 Pm Section RJ Inspection by Lt Ct Renton	1
	30th			4
	31st		Evacuated 10 animals to C/Sgt Barnes & Pte Short S/c 10669 Sgt Stuart AVC reported of Q.V.S. Hopkins to Battalion Henley AVC from 16 DAC. ADDS/Forms/C.2118. aviation, and instructors	3
				2

(Signed) W Renton Lt OC 47th MVS

Army Form C. 2118

WAR DIARY
or
INTELLIGENCE SUMMARY
(Erase heading not required.)

117th Middlesex
Army Veterinary Corps 16 Div June 1916

Instructions regarding War Diaries and Intelligence Summaries are contained in F. S. Regs., Part II. and the Staff Manual respectively. Title pages will be prepared in manuscript.

47th MOBILE SECTION A.V.C. No. 1/1916

Place	Date	Hour	Summary of Events and Information	Remarks and references to Appendices
NIEUX LES MINES	1/6/16		137 others examined by Vet. Sgt (R.A.C) had 3 unwell. May 10 units of the Middlesex Division. Sgt Rake, Pte Chappell to Emergency (Remarks) sick on arrival C13.261. B3270 bad horse, Vet. Hosp. Diagnosis turn. C attached (Shelter etc) Corpl Pte Savage Attached from New Witney Hospital. C132.1 All attached Vergement	admitted 3
	2nd		2 offs, 1 nco, 9 others, 1 horse. Sick parade. Diagnosis Sgt Mears Disposal transit C62396, wound B, 3rd R Cav. Transport lines	2
	3rd		O.R.M. 1 nco sick. Vet Sgt at 9/15/601	4
	4th		Rifle Inspection.	6
	5th		Corpl Wickes C.M. 4162. 1 horse C15.310. Transferred to A. Dep. 117th Field P.Sn. Lieurand Turstin. Vet Major R.N.V.F. 16th Sgt Rooly 9D. 1st Sgt at Veraclem	7
	6th		Transits 12 animals. At Sgt Junket Pte Incas	6
	7th		Sgt Mearn, Cpl Palmer with 1 horse C13.269 to A.1 Field Mound Sect. Venechem. Transitted 8 animals. Cpl M Benson 9/e. M.O.3 Vet trained to 2/Lant Veon (116th Mobi R.S.C.) to carry those types Mare to attention Sgt Rogers Mothered done Oregons C15.302. A.S.M. field attitudes horse C4383 9/Sgt News attachment as Attain	7
	8th		No 5. Hood activities for C6272 v Col. Hodes destroyed at attn. C13.300 attached to Vet Hosp sick. Sgt Rooly 9 (M.C.W.1) returned from rest A.C. Pte Sent R. (111.79.1) transferred to L.B.2 Veterinary Hospital Cities	4
	9th		Tomate 8th animal a P.S.M. Pitlochry dies attack Major Moen arrived	3

2353 Wt W2544/1454 700,000 5/15 D. D. & L. A.D.S.S./Forms/C. 2118.

Army Form C. 2118.

WAR DIARY
or
INTELLIGENCE SUMMARY.

(Erase heading not required.)

4th Mobile Section
A.V.C.

Jan 1916

Instructions regarding War Diaries and Intelligence Summaries are contained in F.S. Regns., Part II. and the Staff Manual respectively. Title pages will be prepared in manuscript.

47th MOBILE SECTION

Place	Date	Hour	Summary of Events and Information	Remarks and references to Appendices
NOEUX LES MINES	10/1/16		6.75.314 destroyed on being P Battery 99th R.F.A. a cartoose taken to Cdr Hagen in float. Pte Col. A.G. (11980) left for England on leave. Plans & tents for Cond of Section.	Attached 3
	11th		O.C. Capt Bey returned from leave. A/Capt Freeman returned.	1
	12th		C.V.S. Met arrived by C.H. Pendleton & S.Peris to front to (attached). Evacuated M. Curnock to E Sgt Hughes with Colic to 33rd F.A. 1/8 men on M.D. Three fehren (1 resort fm H.Q. 2 Divs.) Sec.mg. Col.	11
	13th		Refit. Inspection.	1
	14th		Arrived from General Depot 1 N. 200 dog. Pte C. Hudson & Pte Michael West (attd to A.D.V.S. Choplan(?) M. Coasleys sent to A.D.V.S. (hospital)	4
	15th		Evacuated 13 Animals A/Capt Moore & Pte Barker & Sheep Brooks to leave to Court 2 Loads of dogs.	3
	16th		Time for dog to stay. Pte J. Thomas to Cond'l return to Unit w.o. C.B. 339 & (word?) Ancient whch F. 15/1/16.	5
	17th		Requisition sent New to Come Ltn cold (?) 345.310 Shep hid. Any Corne for 1. Capt Moore & A. Breton returned. Bty Corne Regt & animals for Russian Convoy station. Blacksmith & forge tents & equipment tc also animal place to Exeosnin Convoy station. Put in 2nd of tent dis Chance (took so many dogs). Plans to Chance many for no Line Inspected.	6
	18th		No ledger(?) Pte Queen & 17001. Ratch. to leave to arrange disposal of M.A. Section kits. 1 Police to A.D.V.S. for inspection to meet 2nd in of (illegible) Catering station. Col. Price & Thomas from Leave. C.B.339 held Court (K-nineices).	12

2353 Wt. W2544/1454 700,000 5/15 D.D.& L. A.D.S.S./Forms/C.2118.

Army Form C. 2118.

WAR DIARY
or
INTELLIGENCE SUMMARY.
(Erase heading not required.)

H.Q. Australian Sigs. A.V.C.

June 1916

Instructions regarding War Diaries and Intelligence Summaries are contained in F. S. Regs., Part II. and the Staff Manual respectively. Title pages will be prepared in manuscript.

Place	Date	Hour	Summary of Events and Information	Remarks and references to Appendices
NOEUX LES MINES	19/6/16		[illegible entry]	2.
	20/6/16		[illegible entry]	10.
	21/6/16		[illegible entry]	4.
	22/6/16		[illegible entry]	5.
	23/6/16		[illegible entry]	5.
	24/6/16		[illegible entry]	3.
	25/6/16		[illegible entry]	3.
	26/6/16		[illegible entry]	3.
	27/6/16		[illegible entry]	9.
	28/6/16		[illegible entry]	4.
	29/6/16		[illegible entry]	1/5
	30/6/16		[illegible entry]	6.

W. H. [signature] Capt.
O.C. 4th A.V.C.S.

WAR DIARY

47th Mobile Veterinary
Section AVC.

1st. July to 31st. July 1916.

VOLUME No. 8

Army Form C. 2118.

WAR DIARY
or
INTELLIGENCE SUMMARY.

(Erase heading not required.)

47th Mobile Section
Army Veterinary Corps
16th Division

JULY 1916

Place	Date	Hour	Summary of Events and Information	Remarks and references to Appendices.
Noeux-les-Mines	1.7.16		Evacuated 11 animals. One load of stray drawn for standings.	
	2.7.16		Conducting Party (L.Cpl. Barnes 9c.) Limber brought back from Ordnance Workshops, Lillers-Annere, after repair. Limber borrowed from 142 Co. A.S.C. returned.	
	3/7/16		Conducting Party returned. Stores to Mazingarbe.	
	4/7/16		Two loads of stray drawn for standings.	
	5/7/16		Stores to Hinchin. Limber for 2 loads stray.	
	6th		Nine animals evacuated. Limber for one load manure.	
	7th		Limber to Mazingarbe with for 2 loads stray.	
	8th		Limber for 2 loads stray.	
	10th		22 Animals taken to Station for evacuation but returned on account of bombardment of Railhead.	

WAR DIARY
INTELLIGENCE SUMMARY

47th M.V.S. 16th Division

JULY 1916

Army Form C. 2118.

Place	Date	Hour	Summary of Events and Information	Remarks and references to Appendices
Provenc- Les- Mines	July 11th		23 Animals evacuated. Shoed collected horse from 182 Bde. R.F.A.	
	12th		Rifle inspected & passed by Armourer.	
	13th		12 Animals evacuated. Conducting Party (July 11th) returned. Shoed collected Animal from 180th Bde. R.F.A.	
	14th		Limber to Magnicourt for coal & wood. Shoed to Vandricourt.	
	15th		Evacuation 7. 91 Arrivals. Conducting Party returned.	
	17th		Shoed to 11th Hants. - Animal taken to abattoir & destroyed. Conducting Party returned.	
	18th		22 Animals evacuated.	
	19th		Shoed to Vandricourt. Shoed to Nogin.	
	20th		Conducting Party returned. Shoed to Vandricourt. Steel helmets for 507. J Section issued.	
	21st		12 Animals evacuated. Limber to Magnigade for coal & wood.	
	22nd		Shoed to Hersdigneul at 6.30 pm. - to Noyelles at 11 pm.	
	23rd		Shoed to Noyelles. Men to 112th Field Ambulance.	

Army Form C. 2118.

WAR DIARY
or
INTELLIGENCE SUMMARY.

47th M.V.S.
16th Division
JULY 1916

(Erase heading not required.)

Instructions regarding War Diaries and Intelligence Summaries are contained in F. S. Regs., Part II. and the Staff Manual respectively. Title page will be prepared in manuscript.

Place	Date	Hour	Summary of Events and Information	Remarks and references to Appendices
Nouvelle-Mine	July 25th		Evacuate 21 animals	
	26th		Conducting Party returned. Evacuate 23 animals	
	27th		Float to Vandricourt.	
	28th		Conducting Party returned. Evacuate 14 animals. Limber to Marzingarbe for Cord. Stove to Fosse 3 Philosophe to Timber &c.	
	29th		Stove to 77th Bde R.F.A. for animal (US 623) with Shell Wound - taken to abattoir & destroyed.	
	30th		Conducting Party returned. 8 animals evacuated.	
	31st		Total amount of Liq. Calcis sulphidum made during the month is 117½ gallons.	

W. Winton Capt. A.V.C.
O.C. 47th M.V.S.

Vol 8

WAR DIARY.

44th Mobile Veterinary Section

MONTH OF AUGUST, 1916.

VOLUME:- 9.

Army Form C. 2118.

WAR DIARY
or
INTELLIGENCE SUMMARY.
(Erase heading not required.)

47th MOBILE SECTION
A.V.C.

Place	Date	Hour	Summary of Events and Information	Remarks and references to Appendices
NOEUX LES MINES.	August 1916			
	1st		Conducting Party returned from Kent Chatel.	
	2nd		Evacuated 15 Animals. Sgt. Morgan i/c. Shoeing Smith for 3 teams of Slings.	
	3rd		Capt. Lenton & 12 mounted men of Section went for route march with marching order & full kits	
	4th		Conducting Party returned. Limber to Hazebrouck for Coal & Wood.	
	6th		Float to B/80 — RFA. R.H.A. for C.B. to 65H & thence to Shalom. Animal Nohryn by Sgt. Mason.	
	7th		Evacuation of Animals Re. Ross i/c.	
	8th		Float to B/151 — RFA R.H.A. for C.B. No. 662.	
	9th		Conducting Party returned. C.B. No. 662 taken in charge in front & Nohryn by Sgt. Morgan. Capt. Lenton & 7 horsemen to see sick animal at 76th Rifle School.	

WAR DIARY or INTELLIGENCE SUMMARY

Army Form C. 2118.

47th MOBILE SECTION
A.V.C.

Place	Date	Hour	Summary of Events and Information	Remarks and references to Appendices
NOEUX LES MINES	August 1916 (Continued)			
	10th		Sgt. Morgan & party Manifield Camp Cornett Stables.	
	11th		Evacuated 8 Animals. Pte. Palmer I/c. Marched to Mazingarbe for Coal & Wood. Sgt. Morgan & party continued Manifesting Camp Cornett stables. Limber for 3 Coals of Hay.	
	12th		Cranchy party returned.	
	13th			
	14th		Capt. Hunter A.V.C. supplied with lime & sulphur for 15 Epsom L.G.S. (Enc.) Limber for chalk & fact lime. Pte. Palmer & Roo to Capt. Reid's stable (R.A. Normansis) to Manifest stables.	
	15th		Evacuated 10 Animals. Pte Hopkins & Horner I/c. Limber for 5r con of hay.	
		4.30 pm	Sgt. Coppin from 11 R. Stables (P.) arrived & men overnight. Horse wagons & 13 N.C. 683 & took mules to return for concentration.	
	16th		Sgt. Coppin received orders to strain matters ready, & expand to open with at 6 p.m.	

WAR DIARY or INTELLIGENCE SUMMARY

Army Form C. 2118.

Place	Date	Hour	Summary of Events and Information	Remarks and references to Appendices
NOEUX LES MINES	Aug 1916 (Continued)			
	16th		Pte. Marchington E. Kicker in face (Y. 30 min.) & taken to M.S. Field Amb. & Evacuated to C.C.S. (Ref. 111th J. Amb. E2393)	
	17th		G.B.2:° 691 colicked by float from Headquarters. Evacuated 8 Horses (Pte. Lucas & Spare) Y/C. Conveying Party returned	
	18th		Went to A.V.V. 2nd. R.H.A. In G.B.2° 69H, taken to stables 9 destroyed by Sgt Mason. Handed in magnets for costs a word. Similar for "Ennis" Slug.	
	19th		Conveying Party returned.	
	21st		Evacuated 8 animals Re. Spare Y/C. Supplied D18th Rn R.H.A. with 16 spare Great.	
	22nd		Evacuated 3 Animals by Barge from Bethune at 6 am. Similar for 2 Loads of Hay. Pte. Rea to D18th Rn R.H.A. to disinfect stalls. Evacuated 5 Animals to Rept. Closh by tram, Rte. Lucas Y/C.	

Army Form C. 2118.

WAR DIARY
or
INTELLIGENCE SUMMARY.
(Erase heading not required.)

Place	Date	Hour	Summary of Events and Information	Remarks and references to Appendices
NOEUX LES MINES	Aug. 1916 23rd		Conducting Clerk returned. Sgt Morgan & party completed stables at D 180 & 73m R.H.A. Left for C.B. No. Y/28. A/141 73rd R.H.A. Went to 16th Div: Horse (Mericourt) for C.B. No. Y/24.	
	24th		Evacuated 6 animals by Barge from Bethune. Conducting party returned from Rest Chateau. C.B. No. Y/21 taken to Abattoir & destroyed by Capt. Moon.	
	25th		Evacuated 15 animals by train to Rest Chateau. Pte Barnes & Lucas I/C. Rejoined at Hesdigneul 13 noon. Gen. Advance party (Cpl Godfrey & Pte Osborne) left Noeux for new quarters at Equenedeuing with mule & cart.	
	26th 8am		Men from Osborne & B.S. supply wagon joined rehrn echelon. Echelon left Noeux les Mines. Left Sgt Bradford T. A.V.C. from 15th M.V.S. who took over primus & angelin stove. Rear Guard (Cpl Taylor & Pte Montague & Blackburn) found horn lorry on road. Return taken on road for an hour to make a feed.	

Army Form C. 2118.

WAR DIARY
or
INTELLIGENCE SUMMARY.
(Erase heading not required.)

Instructions regarding War Diaries and Intelligence Summaries are contained in F. S. Regs., Part II. and the Staff Manual respectively. Title pages will be prepared in manuscript.

Place	Date	Hour	Summary of Events and Information	Remarks and references to Appendices
HAYE, ECQUEDECQUES	August 1916			
	26th	2.30 p.m.	Arrived (Map Ref. V15a 2¼ Map 36A.) Drew 10 rations each. Tobacco.	
	27th		Rifles Ecquedecques 11.30 a.m. Ph. Palmer to no. 1 Vetrin Remounts, GONNEHEM, for charge for A.D.V.S. Sanitary party returned from Rest Camp (8 Other Ranks).	
	28th		Sgt. Thealer A.V.C. no 10669 arrived for reporting. Sgt. Herst A.V.C. no 8309 arrived for reporting. Sgt. Ivula A.V.C. no 9233 " " "	
	29th		SE 3194 OR Long L. A.V.G. arrived from no. 9 Very Hospital. Sgt. Streaks which very & Mnt Chop Veh. Sandu on h Sgt. Woolley A.V.G.	A.V.G.
	30th	10.30 a.m.	Kehin left Haye, Ecquedecques, marched to LILLERS, Ration Strength. Forenoon 19 animals from Ration in charge of 3 A.V.C. Sgt. marcher on to received entrainment orders en to proceed to no. 7 Very Hospt. LE HAVRE.	
SAILEUX	31st	3 pm	Train left LILLERS arrived SAILEUX 10.30 p.m.	
		5 am	Detrained, breakfasted & left 8 am. March to DAOURS arrived 5 p.m. Both Ration immediately to NEUVIETE. Billeted. Draw rations (NOEUX LES MINES 4) Army Fhy 24 Gallons.	W Newton Capt MC OC 47 M.V.S.

WAR DIARY

14th Mobile Veterinary Section

FOR MONTH OF SEPTEMBER, 1916.

VOLUME

Army Form C. 2118.

WAR DIARY
or
INTELLIGENCE SUMMARY.
(Erase heading not required.)

Place	Date	Hour	Summary of Events and Information	Remarks and references to Appendices
	Sep			
DAOURS	3	—	Capt. Howe A.V.C. O.D. between attached to Section. Broke camp at 11 a.m., leaving rear party, Corpl. Godfrey & one man c/o 4 sick animals. Arrived at MORLANCOURT 7 p.m.	
MORLANCOURT	4th	—	Supply wagon to EDGEHILL for rations 1 p.m. Evacuated (collecting station established at CITADEL) — 1 Sergt A.V.C., 3 men A.V.C., one driver A.S.C. with forces; the between reaches Capt. Howe A.V.C. chiversiste with food.	
	5th	—	Left at 4 p.m., marched to ARRBG FOURCHÉ reaching there 6 p.m.	
ARRBG FOURCHÉ	6th	—	Drew rations at GROVE TOWN Station.	
	7th	—	Shoed for O.B.782.	
	8th	—	Evacuated 16 animals from GROVE TOWN. Shod for O3790.	
	9th	—	Evacuated 41 animals. Adv. Coll. 9 Sqn withdrawn from CITADEL rejoined section 4 p.m. Vans conveying section remained.	
	10th	—	Evacuated 8 animals. Handed over to 1/14 London M.V.S. 4 carts.	
	11th	—	Left ARRBG FOURCHÉ at 8 a.m. arriving Sailey-le-SEC 11.30 a.m. Evacuated 3 animals. Handed over to 1/11 London M.V.S. 4 carts.	

WAR DIARY or INTELLIGENCE SUMMARY

Army Form C. 2118.

Place	Date	Hour	Summary of Events and Information	Remarks and references to Appendices
	Sep			
	12th	8 a.m.	Left Camp 8 a.m., arrived SAILLY-LE-SEC 11.30 a.m. Two conducting parties returned. Capt. Howe A.V.C. & Parmers to 47th Inf. Bde.	
SAILLY-LE-SEC	16th		Evacuated 5 animals from MÉRICOURT L'ABBÉ	
	17th	2.30 p.m.	Left at 2.30 p.m. & marched via CORBIE, DAOURS, AMIENS, LONGPRÉ, ST SAUVEUR to TIRANCOURT, halting 5.30 to 6.30 p.m. at DAOURS to water Team & arriving at TIRANCOURT at 1.30 a.m. 18.9.16. Pte Florence fell out sick, after leaving CORBIE & was sent back to C.C.S. at Corbie. 7 animals were evacuated from CORBIE en route.	
TIRANCOURT	18th	1.30 a.m.	Arrived 1.30 a.m. camped in road-side. Left TIRANCOURT at 10 a.m. & arrived at AIRAINES at 4 p.m. & bivouac in Rue de COURCHON.	
AIRAINES	20th		Two conducting parties returned. Sgt Morgan & 4 men to Abbeville to draw remounts. Orderly to Hellencourt & Allerville per remount. Shoe. S. Corpl. Taylor to LIMEUX for sick animal.	
AIRAINES	21st		Pte Palmer to Abbeville with wounded no. 7 animals left with Horse Recovery Post. I at Café de...	

Army Form C. 2118.

WAR DIARY
or
INTELLIGENCE SUMMARY.
(Erase heading not required.)

Instructions regarding War Diaries and Intelligence Summaries are contained in F.S. Regs., Part II. and Staff Manual respectively. Title pages will be prepared in manuscript.

4TH MOBILE SECTION
No. III
Date Sept 15 1916
A.V.C.

Place	Date	Hour	Summary of Events and Information	Remarks and references to Appendices
	Sep		Ru Paire, Rue du Couchon, Aisnes. Rejoined Section at Longpré	
LONGPRÉ	21st		Left Aisnes at 4.30 p.m. Arriving at Longpré 6.35 p.m. Watered & fed & entrained 8.30 p.m. Train left at 11.1 p.m.	
GODEWAERSVELDE	Sep 22nd		Arrived at Godewaersvelde at 8 a.m., left at 9 a.m. & marched to S.2.2.9.8. Arriving at 2 p.m.	
MEULEHOUCK	23	—	Supply wagon to Wippenhoek for supplies. Horse to 48th M. Gun Co. for sick animal. H.D. 144 C. A.S.C. left with 10th Bde. C.F.A. taken to 910 C.M.V.S.	
Mont Rouge (M.15.d.7.3)	24th	—	Left camp at 8 a.m. marched to Mont Rouge (M.15.d.7.3) Took over 12 animals & Camp from 2nd C.M.V.S.. H.D. J144Co. A.S.C. destroyed & burnt.	
	25th	—	C.B. 885 - taken to abattoir at BAILLEUL. Tried to induce Glad mich 2 sick animals (two trips) to Wippenhoek, when they were left with one man ready for evacuation.	
	26th		Evacuated by special train 7 animals - all unpurchased.	
	27th		Horse to 9th Bde. C.F.A. pr CB. 971; to abattoir Bailleul with CB. 889. Two trips to IX Corps Cavalry for CBs No.s 968 & 969	
	28th		1 Cpl., 1 L/Cpl. & 8 men J/ 3 C.D.A.C. attached to Section for duty. Pte. Trud (conducting duty 26th) returned.	

WAR DIARY or INTELLIGENCE SUMMARY

Army Form C. 2118.

Place	Date	Hour	Summary of Events and Information	Remarks and references to Appendices
	Sep			
Mont Rouge (M.15.d.7.3)	29th		Evacuated 39 animals by road to S.P. Dnes. Sgt Morgan, ten men J.M.V.S. & Sick man 1 C.D.A.C. as conducting party. Animals were sent in strings of twelve & P. Paire - Sick Paire in a strong, with one man leading two pair, One, The front pair & me the last pair. Pte. Colonel & Free admitted to 111th Field Ambulance. L/Cpl & Sick man 3 C.D.A.C. returned to Coys. Road to abatoir, Bailleul, via C.15.9.16.	
	30th		Locre for C.15.9.77.	

A. Smith Capt. R.A.V.C.
O.C. 47th M.V.S.

WAR DIARY

MONTH OF OCTOBER, 1916.

VOLUME 11

H.Q. Mobile Veterinary Section

Vol 10

Army Form C. 2118.

47th MOBILE SECTION, A.V.C.

WAR DIARY or INTELLIGENCE SUMMARY.

(Erase heading not required.)

Instructions regarding War Diaries and Intelligence Summaries are contained in F.S. Regs., Part II. and the Staff Manual respectively. Title pages will be prepared in manuscript.

Place	Date	Hour	Summary of Events and Information	Remarks and references to Appendices
WESTOUTRE	1st	11am	Pte min 3rd C.R.C.S. returned in Horse Ambulance of 23 B.V.H. St.OMER from Evacuating Party arrived 19.9.16	
		2pm	Cpl. & 6 Ptes. from horse section C.R.A.S. returned to unit	
			Went to No. 2 Br. C.R.A.S. for lumber & draw a wagon for C.E.S. no. 960.	
	2nd	11.30pm	Lumber to Armour & A.D.V.S's office for Keg of sulphur.	
			" 3rd C.R.A.S. for cement	
			Sgt. & 9 men — Evacuating Party returned from St.OMER — reported loss of one sick animal — "skittle" en route exhaustion. also death of one Mule (Action Horse).	
		S.E. 3.30 Pte. TRENT B. returned from 112th Field Amb.	
		S.E. 11.10 Pte. CORBOULD N. transferred from No. 1 to 16th Ambs. Rest Camp	
			Pte. new from 3rd C.R.A.D. returned to unit	
			Went to C.V.A. for C.I.S. No. 5.	
	3rd		Lumber team to Br. R.A.S. for E.S. Wagon hauled over to 2nd H.M.A.S. Removed mule	
			loan at R.L. proper Gans from Rub.	
			Ote. with Coach truck to C.R.A.E. for 3 bags Cement.	
			Commenced looking at Run Horse Mockings.	

WAR DIARY or INTELLIGENCE SUMMARY

Army Form C. 2118.

Place	Date	Hour	Summary of Events and Information	Remarks and references to Appendices
VESTOUTRE.	October 1916 (continued)			
	4th		Evacuated Pte ammunds by Road from BAILLEUL - 3 men in Embarking Party. R.E. Wagon up & pkts to R.E. & grd. Pte Robb, Birn, Jones, & Knox Rjoined. for transfer of time to R.E. Morris. Went to Ordnance for Steel Ropes, Chains re.	
	5th		512 Cpl ROSS N. & 112th Field Amb for Medical Inspection (Stomach Complaint for) Wagon for 3 cross-band saw or wood trending material.	
	6th		Pte OSBOUND W. returned from 18th Bn Rest Camp. Wagon for 3 cross-band saw or case of bricks. Sgt Rim arrived from M.V. Hants. (Review) & rejoined in execution of Stables. Pte Ross from 154 Field Amby R.D. 1 Entails Hill Klein. Embarking Party returned.	
	7th		S.E. 6345 - Pte HOPKINS A.E. admitted to 718th Field Amb. Wagon for cross-band timber & cross-band tools &c. 2 Pers with Quick Mill to FOCRE invalids Selection from Remounts.	
	8th	9 am	S.E. 8893 Shoeing Smith SPILLER G arrived from N.O. H B.V.H. CALAIS to replace	
		11 am	S.E. 940 " " MOORES A.E. transferred to --- do ---	

Army Form C. 2118.

WAR DIARY
or
INTELLIGENCE SUMMARY.
(Erase heading not required.)

Instructions regarding War Diaries and Intelligence Summaries are contained in F. S. Regs., Part II. and the Staff Manual respectively. Title pages will be prepared in manuscript.

47th MOBILE SECTION, A.V.C. 3

Place	Date	Hour	Summary of Events and Information	Remarks and references to Appendices
WESTOUTRE.	October 1916. (Contd)			
	9th	2.30 pm	Limber for 1st Corps. Sant. Wagon for Fd. Amb. Bread.	
		4/11.15 pm	Went with cart truck to B.W.H. 75th R.F.A. for C.V.S. Lt. 24.	
	10th	8 am	Wagon to Ordnance for V.S. Stores &c.	
			Limber for 1st Corps Food.	
			Wagon for 1 Corps Div. Amm. Club & Conducting Party.	
	11th		S.E. 11410 Pte. CORSRAID W.S. evacuated to S.C.C. Sm.	
			Pte. from 11th Hamb. (R.) attached admitted to 113th Field Amb.	
			Wagon for load of building materials.	
			Limber for 3 Corps Food.	
	12th		Sgt. Linton & Cpl. Thompson to B/87-R.F.A. 3 Animals 6.8 to 21/r. 28 water to Abeele destroyed	
			Vet. to WESTERN to collect G.A. no. 79 — later run over by Supply tractor	
	13th		Limber for 3 tops Tank. Wagon for boot. Building materials & Gas M of Food. Orderly for top of rink	
			Evacuated 28 animals by train from WIPPENHOEK. Sgt. Terryn & Chan. Conducting Party.	
			C.B. No. 24 Pte. M. Walker slight	
	14th		Captain SEXTON acting for A.D.V.S. during his absence on leave.	
			Conducting Party chased.	
			(Continued)	

1577 Wt. W10791/1773 500,000 1/15 D.D. & L. A.D.S.S./Forms/C. 2118.

Army Form C. 2118.

47th MOBILE SECTION, A.V.C.

WAR DIARY
or
INTELLIGENCE SUMMARY.
(Erase heading not required.)

Instructions regarding War Diaries and Intelligence Summaries are contained in F. S. Regs., Part II. and the Staff Manual respectively. Title pages will be prepared in manuscript.

Place	Date	Hour	Summary of Events and Information	Remarks and references to Appendices
NESTOUTRE	October 1916		(Continued)	
	14th		Wagon to EN CAMPE for load of Chips for beds of Cont. from Stab. Limber for load of Sand. Went to R.O.B. for C/S. R.P. 36. Wagon to Kembs for Sand.	
	15th	12 noon	Capt. Carter to BAILLEUL to inspect evacuation.	
		2 pm	Capt. Wilson to Dump at Fort Rept to inspect animals. (16 sure + M.V.S.) Return. A.D.V.S. arrives M.V.S. to work under A.D.V.S. orders. Wagon for Coal Forest. Limber worked. Went to TACRE for C/S. R.P. 38. Captain Carter to A.D.V.S. office, NESTOUTRE. R/S. R.P. 35 return Bailleul Bailleul - airstrip.	
	16th		Captain Carter to inspect animals of 7/8th R.S. Horn & 2/Royal Scot Reg. Limber for at Leeds Bank. Went to 10th B.F. for C/S. R.P. 38.	
	17th		512 Pte Ross N. to BAILLEUR (transport from 13.10.16 to 24 SEAFORTH HIGHLANDERS, authority DRS CRNO 38973 H.S.) to proceed to ETAPLES. Limber for H Cross Sand. Wagon to Carpey winner for 3 saddle Rests. Arms & trucks Rooms. Bake Carter to A.D.Y.S. Office, NESTOUTRE.	
	19th		SE 81194 Pte KING W.C. arrived for reinforcement from hes at BVH. Limber for 2 Cross Sand as Bent worth. Wagon for butting materials to R.O.B. No. 38? Return to Abattoir. SR. 10 NEV. Destroyed.	

WAR DIARY
or
INTELLIGENCE SUMMARY.

Army Form C. 2118.

47th MOBILE SECTION, A.N.Z.

Place	Date	Hour	Summary of Events and Information	Remarks and references to Appendices
WESTOUTRE	OCTOBER 1916		(Continued)	
	20th	9am	The Patrols left as present divided boy went to 33rd A.N.S. BETHUNE to relieve G.S. Lt. Y/O.	
			Links to Bethune for 3 Cross bars.	
			Bgt. Barton and Dies office (Returns.) Wagon for form.	
			Landon & Wagon for Bank (+ men each)	
	21st		Capt. Hunter moved in Materials 18th M.T. CYCL.	
	22nd		Pte. Patrie returned from BETHUNE with G.S. Lt. Y/O.	
			Landon to Materials to for 3 cross vans.	
	23rd		Sgt. Morgan took Lander Wagon to BAILLEUL for trials which have not arrived.	
			Landon for Bail. Lowery. Wagon to LOCRE (ammn) for Oil Drops.	
			West (Armr) to G.S. Lt. Y2 & No 43.	
	24th		S.E. 1/22. Ptes. SAYERS & [?] allotted to weapon mech.	
			Capt. Barton to BAILLEUL to inspect Reservists. On loan and returned.	
			G.S. Lt. Landon to LOCRE.	
	25th		Wagon to D.A.C. for Renneltha Pte. Knapenh. & to hut of building into	
			Word to NIPPEWASSE at 6 am with 15 armies & 2 carriages &c.	
			It came from 11 A.m.b. (?) Minister to met. One Airplane returns from his land.	

WAR DIARY or INTELLIGENCE SUMMARY

Army Form C. 2118.

4/1th MOBILE SECTION, A.V.C. No. 6

Place	Date	Hour	Summary of Events and Information	Remarks and references to Appendices
WESTOUTRE	October 1916 (Continued)			
	26th		Remainder HH Ordnance by rail from NIPPENHOEK. Sgt Harper + 5 Ors. as conducting party. Limbers for sand.	
	27th	9am	Party B. R.D.V.S. officer and wagon for 80th Bn RFA. Conducting party formed. Limbers & wagon for sand. Limber wagon for 8 loads road metal. Limber wagon for 161 Genevre bricks.	
	28th		Limber for 3 loads sand.	
	29th		Wagon to R.E. Kemmel for removal of Klimate etc. Wagon to R.E. Kyans for load of trekking material for mine shaft.	
	30th		Wagon for 2 loads Artaise for shaft + for 50 bundles fascines for road. Limbers for H. Signal Road. Horse to Abelaar BANKEUR with O.C. No. W/1 + 48.	
		11.30p	Capt. Kenton to LOCRE to obtain Recorts at 5 pm.	
	31st		Limber for 50 Ridds. fascines - 1 load sand + road metal. Wagon for Strays Club (3) H. sand. S/S 1/129 Pte SQUIRES transferred 79/20. 1 Section C. E. S. Captain Kenton to LOCRE to obtain sealed tubes.	
			Fig. CPLC SMITH Had a round during October:- 199 Rations	Signature Capt OC "4.11."

WAR DIARY.

FOR

MONTH OF NOVEMBER, 1916.

VOLUME 12.

No. 47. Mobile Vety Section

Vol XI

Army Form C. 2118.

WAR DIARY
or
INTELLIGENCE SUMMARY.
(Erase heading not required.)

47th Mobile Section
A.V.C.
16th Division

November 1916

47th MOBILE SECTION, A.V.C.
No. O.88
Date 7/12/16

Place	Date	Hour	Summary of Events and Information	Remarks and references to Appendices
WESTOUTRE	Nov 1st/16	9.0 am	Limbers to Mont Noir for 50 Bundles Fascines & 2 loads sand for roadmaking. G.S. Wagon to R.E. Yard for material for building hut for men. Went to 49th Fd. Co. for animal C13.90. One animal C13.88 destroyed & buried. Capt Renton to Locre to give final lecture on stable management. Capt Renton on leave to England.	4 animals admitted
	2nd	—	Pte Martin R. No. 819 A.V.C. arrived at Bailleul Station as reinforcement, from No. 2 Veterinary Hospital. Met by Pte Palmer with spare horse & saddle. Limber to Mont Noir for 50 Fascines & 2 loads sand. G.S. Wagon for hut flooring.	3 animals admitted
	3rd	9.40	Wagon for straw & to R.E's for tools & man to erect hut for section. Limber for Capt Howes kit to DE 20N CAMP. Limber for 1 load sand. Orderly Room 11347 Pte Winkley R. awarded 14 Days F.P. No 1. Sent under escort to A.P.M. 31817 Dvr Smith J. R.F.A. (Capt Howes Batman) attached to Section. Evacuated 11 Animals by Barge from Bqc. ST MAUR.	
	4th	—	Wagon to Canada Corner for load of Straw. Lorry Wagon & limber for 2 loads sand each. Limber to BAILLEUR. Cpl Jay for Dinner & Pte for 500 Bricks for stalls.	
	5th	—	Wagon & limber to BAILLEUR for 500 Bricks. Pte Hopkins & Pte. Rapture (?) on leave are buried.	1 animal admitted

Army Form C. 2118.

47th Mobile Section A.V.C.

47th Mobile Section A V C War Diary or Intelligence Summary
16th Div.

Place	Date	Hour	Summary of Events and Information	Remarks and references to Appendices
WESTOUTRE	Nov 6/1916	7th	Limber for 50 Fascines, Wagon for 1 load of straw	
	7th	Limber Wagon for 2 loads sand each. 6 animals admitted	6 animals admitted
	8th	1000 Bricks from Bailleul to Peterborough dumped at nearest point, brought on Section premises by Limber Wagon. No. 8983 Pte Breeze W. V.A.V.C. arrangement from 82 Veterinary Hospital	1 animal admitted
	9th	Limber for 50 Fascines Wagon for 2 loads sand, Limber for logs	15 animals admitted
	10th	Limber for Coal wood 1 load for animal CB N.24 Wagon for 1 and 2 loads Limber for 50 Fascines Wagon for holding Material Straw Limber for 3 loads of Sand Gravel	6 animals admitted
		No. 2747 Pte Surtagee granted leave to England Nov 1st - 15 - 21st	1 animal admitted
	11th	Limber for 2 loads sand 50 fascines. Wagon for straw	1 animal admitted
	12th	Evacuated 18 animals by Rail. Lt R Ryan & Pte Trent NCO Limber to Ordnance	10 animals admitted
	13th	Host to SHAEKTEN for animal CB 114.	1 animal admitted
		Wagon for load of Rd Chips 1 load of straw Limber for Ordnance 2nd Lt R Ryan & Pte Trent returned	1 animal admitted
	14th	Limber for Coal wood 1 ole one load of sand one of Gravel. Host Collected CB 119 Capt Hendoe returned from leave	1 animal admitted
	15th	Evacuated 1 animal by train to A.O.M.F.R. Pte Palmer I/C Limber for Rd Chips 1 load of Gravel 1 one of Sand	1 animal admitted

Army Form C. 2118.

WAR DIARY
47th Mobile Section A.V.C. INTELLIGENCE SUMMARY

(Erase heading not required.)

November 1916

Place	Date	Hour	Summary of Events and Information	Remarks and references to Appendices
WESTOUTRE	Nov 16/16		Wagon for Rations. Wagon for R.L Props. Limber for Rations. Start for CB 132. Sgt Nelson on leave to England Nov 17th to 27th	2 animals admitted
	17th		Wagon for Gravel Sand. Limber for Rations Land. Pte Palmer returned	
	18th		Wagon for loads of Shaw sand, & Gravel, Limber for Gravel Sand. CB 125 taken to Attention by Cpl Godfrey	Pte animals admitted
	19th		Evacuated 19 Animals from Wytschaete to Rail. Capt Lenton to Neuf Chatel. Horses Cpl Saye on Pte Hopkins to Pte Palmer conducting party. CB 123 dead carcase buried	3 animals admitted
	20th		Pte Hayworth returned from 112th Field Ambulance. Limber for Rations & Gravel. Wagon for building material & R.L Props. Pte Marston admitted into 112th Field Ambulance. CB 125 + 132 Derobigen to Attention.	
	21st		Limber for Coal wood & load of sand. Wagon for sand & Gravel. Dvr Hoforth admitted into 112th Field Ambulance & Evacuated to No 1 C.C.S for dental treatment. Pte Palmer returned from Neuf Chatel by Road. Capt Lenton	1 animal admitted

Army Form C. 2118.

47 Mobile Section WAR DIARY or
A.V.C. INTELLIGENCE SUMMARY
16th Div

(Erase heading not required.)

Place	Date	Hour	Summary of Events and Information	Remarks and references to Appendices
Wadelincourt	Nov 22nd/16		Wagon for Gravel. Sawren, Limber for land Gravel. Pte Palmer attached to 112th S.Y. Amb. Champ. from 47th Inf S Bde to assist in hutmaking. Morning The Bleak for CRS 144	2 animals admitted
	23rd		Flood collected CRS.R 142+146. Limber for cut wood. Wagon for Brass Engal. & 142/20 Workshop from 142 Dade reinforcement. Cpl Godfry to Lawns 1405) Dr Smith B (Sic) to 13/17 Bde R.F.A. working at 200 F.S. Mt b.	5 horses admitted
	24th		The Gunners returned from Lawn. Wagon to RE Dupts Gravel. Limber for Gravel Land.	22 animals admitted
	25th		Wagon for RE Dupts, Engineers II animals from Westwork Prickly S/C Limber for Beauchamp for Queens. Harness cleaning S/c	1 animal admitted
	26th		Old Stable returned	
	27th		Wagon to Boscholes for Queens. Limber for that for Lines of Comm of Eupal back Cpl Begley & Pony to Bailleul for 3000 Bricks to be used in Cooler Service.	15 animals admitted
	28th		Flood for Sausome Gump. Limber carrying bricks on to Sisters Quarters	
	29th		Dr Hyath returned from R.A.C.C.S. Cpl Cowan returned from leave. 2nd Wagon Sent by Lieut Grew to Stores. Limber carting bricks. Flood for Sausome. Pte Sandys on leave to England.	15 animals admitted
	30th		Limber for 3 loads sand. Flood for RE Dupts.	5 animals admitted

W. Newton
Capt A.V.C.
O.C. 47th M.V.S.

WAR DIARY FOR MONTH OF DECEMBER, 1916.

VOLUME B

47th Mobile Veterinary Section

Army Form C. 2118.

WAR DIARY
or
INTELLIGENCE SUMMARY.

(Erase heading not required.)

Dec/1916.

47th Mobile Section A.V.C. 16 Dec[?]

47th MOBILE SECTION, A.V.C.
O264
Date 3/12/16

Place	Date	Hour	Summary of Events and Information	Remarks and references to Appendices
WESTOUTRE	Dec 1/16		Total of Sigt Allis Sulph. Concentrated made and issued trunks during November 37 Galvs.	Summary Attached
		9am.	Sgt Runyan and 5 men to Bac St Maur with 9 animals for evacuation to St Omer by barge	1
		11am	Cpl Taylor with float to BAILLEUL conveying OB:144 to Batchar limber. Two takes of sand from R.S. Bakery	
	Dec 2nd	2pm	Capt Renton and Sgt Runyan to DAC for forage and issuing of 96 remounts	3
		3pm	Wagon to Canada Corner for fit props for road making	
			Limber for coal & wood	
	3rd	9.30am	Cpl Taylor and five men to meet Lorries at Westoutre proceed to Steenvoorde for issuing	2
			to 211 General's Stabs for section Stables	
			Sgt Chappell to 8th Dublins with animal OB 171 Cased and issued	
	4th	6.am.	9926 Pte King J. B.C. to Railhead Station 7.30 tram to ETAPLES, transferred to hospital horse section of	3
			Empl Service Coy. Pte Ranson to hospitals horse sick.	
			Brancher Kenneth to ST OMER by road Sgt Runyan and 3 men etc.	
		9.30	Cpl Taylor & men to Westoutre to Rail by Lorries to Steenvoorde for issuing of 240 animals	
			Cash for section Stables	
		4pm	Sgt W.H. Busch Horsies farm LA CLYTE to collect sick animal, transportation 8pm could not travel	
			till received ... rupt Pte Palmer W.C.S. 47th. D.T. transferred from 112 K. Stadt L. to 15 Vet. Battalion	
	5th	7.30 am	Sgt Punt to 3 others to Westoutre to travel by Lorry to Steenvoorde for purpose of issuing completion of Stabs 49.	1
			Horse & Pack Horsies farm to Rollestrainier OB 194. Cpl Taylor sick and 1st LA CLYTE and	
			treated same.	
			Shell having only vehicle available to remove sick to war cases	
			Issued on Army Section wood staff from scrap dump on to section Stores/ay.	
			OB 183 received Pte Ross ? 91116 b/Dvy Horton D.C. Battalion has been transferred from 112 K. Stadt L. to 15 Vet. Rail Station	

W.L.

Army Form C. 2118.

WAR DIARY Dec 1916.
or
INTELLIGENCE SUMMARY. 47th Mobile Section A.V.C.
16th Division

(Erase heading not required.)

47th MOBILE SECTION, A.V.C.
No. ....
Date: 1/1/17

Instructions regarding War Diaries and Intelligence Summaries are contained in F.S. Regs., Part II. and the Staff Manual respectively. Title pages will be prepared in manuscript.

Place	Date	Hour	Summary of Events and Information	Remarks and references to Appendices
WESTOUTRE	Dec 6/16.		24 corrugated iron sheets from sides of sheds & section sheds to be reconstructed. Carried Wagon to Canada Corner. Lt Simmons present. Sgt Morgan sparts ff 3 men returned from St Omer. 2 horses as loaders for two brown wagons lent by A.S.C. for gravel.	Animals admitted 3
	7th	8.30 am	Wagon for view timber for road washes. Camada Comer. Pte Grant as driver.	
		9.0 am	Float to BOESCHEPE for animal C/3/198 Lym Winkelhulen proceeding on leave. Pushing to BAILLEUL STAT. to bring animals home that Wagon carting concrete slats from road dump to section premises	1
	8th	2 am	Sgt Morgan to WIPPENHOEK Siding to meet A.D.V.S. and assist in detraining & removing of remounts.	
		9.30 am	Float to BAILLEUL conveying animal C/3/198 to be examined from there by motor Ambulance to Veterinary Hospital ST OMER. Another journey 11.30am with animal C/21/94 for same hospital.	8
		2 pm	2 Privates as loaders for two wagons of gravel.	
		1.30 pm	Cpl Taylor & 2 Ptes to SCHAEXKEN for loading two wagons with bricks from a derelict house standing in emplacement; walls with O.C. Remount Farm. Sun loan of 4 Lt Wynn. Knows retrieves these to proceed to on alternate days to SCHAEXKEN for old bricks, on other days 2 to SCHAEXKEN and 2 to R.E. QUARRY for gravel. Section to provide 2 loaders daily.	
		2pm	2 wagons for gravel. 2pm Float to 17 Bde CoH for sick animals. Pte Palmer returned from 16th Dev Post Station returned to duty.	
	9th	1.30pm	Cpl Taylor & 4 Ptes to SCHAEXKEN for 4 loads old bricks. Limbed carting bricks on to road, hand & Lt Wynn to 4 horses. 2 Drivers also two journeys to road dump for concrete slats 15' each load.	W. 2
	10th		Similar carting bricks from road dump to section premises possible.	

Army Form C. 2118.

WAR DIARY Dec 1916
or
INTELLIGENCE SUMMARY. 47th Mobile Section AVC
16th Division
(Erase heading not required.)

47th MOBILE SECTION, A.V.C.
No. 0
Date 1/1/17

Place	Date	Hour	Summary of Events and Information	Remarks and references to Appendices
WESTOUTRE	Dec 11th/16	1-30	Wagon to Canada Corner for Straw, Cement, & Oiled linen. Cpl Taylor & 2 men to ISHAEKKEN for 2 loads old bricks. 2 Rfn for 2 loads of Gravel. Limber Waggon carting old bricks + cements slabs from road dump. Capt Carter & Pte Palmer to BERTHEN to collect from inhabitants 2 horse toys by 106th +109th Bgd RFA.	Animals Admitted 2
12th		1-30	Pte Hopkins to BAILLEUL for dental treatment. Limber to Ordnance for Chaff duster etc. Cpl Taylor +4 men for 4 loads bricks from ISHAEKKEN	2
13th		9.10am	Evacuated 20 animals by rail (other five taken to WIPPENHOEK SIDING by truck) all transferred to N°23 Hospital ST OMER. 4 AVC plumes S/c. Pte Hopkins to BAILLEUL for further dental treatment.	
		10.am	Pte Savage returned from leave	
		1-30pm	Cpl Taylor +2 men to ISHAEKKEN for 2 trucks bricks. 2 men for 2 loads Gravel.	1
		9am	L/Cpl Rowland arrived from 157 Agricl CoyRB for Slab-laying work, one day only	
14th		1-30pm	Limber carting old bricks on ground. Wagon carting slabs 4/Section premises	
		3pm	Sgt Manson +4 men to LAHAEKKEN for 4 loads old bricks	
			L/Cpl Rowland Rec'd G returned from ST OMER.	1
15th		1-30pm	Pte Queen Pioneer leave to England Dec 16th C.26.H. Sgt Morgan +2 men for two loads bricks. 2 men for two loads gravel. Wagon to BOESCHEPE for Straw. Limber to CANADA CORNER for coal work Pte Martin as driver	
16th		9pm	L/Cpl Whitlow arrived from 157 th S.Co. R.E. for Slab laying. Asst to N°1 Co O.C. (manned C.B. 219 Pte Hopkins to BAILLEUL for further dental treatment. Belgian Civilian arrived to report for L/Cpl Whitlow in slab laying. Wagon to Canada Corner for timber + bricks. Limber Lightly loaded on return Sgt Morgan +2 men to BERTHEN for 4 loads old bricks returned from 16th Division A.V.C.	2
		1-30pm 6pm		

Lieut Blackburn Veterinary Officer in charge 8pm Divisional A.V.C. returned from 16 Div Rail Station

Army Form C. 2118

WAR DIARY Dec. 1916.
or
INTELLIGENCE SUMMARY. 47 Mobile Section A.V.C.
16th Division

(Erase heading not required.)

Instructions regarding War Diaries and Intelligence Summaries are contained in F. S. Regs., Part II and the Staff Manual respectively. Title pages will be prepared in manuscript.

47th MOBILE SECTION A.V.C.
No. 9
Date: 1/1/17

Place	Date	Hour	Summary of Events and Information	Remarks and references to Appendices
WESTOUTRE	Dec 17/12/16		The King granted leave to England Dec 18th to 28th. The Piece to bring sick & lame horses from Belm. Battalion transport. Driver selection all on harness, saddlery, cleaning. Transform 177th Bde R.F.A. at 16th D.A.C. trough for horses, and instructed to stay overnight to assist in conveying sick animals to Base on the 18th. 46 Collar section to carry on road mending	Animals Admitted 15
	Dec 18th		Evacuated 18 Animals to ST. OMER by road. Sgt. Morgan i/c with Pte. Palmer Chappell A.V.C. Driver of 177th Bde a 1 of D.A.C. Lumber cart + pack Mule. Shot to 7th Siege RSA for CB 236. La/ftcer 1 to VLAMERTINGHE to collect animal CB 227 of 162 Canadian tunnelling Co. L/Cpl. Rolland of 157th S.O. R.G. recalled from Belgian Durham & dying on account of a Private for ant. dying ? Pte. Parcer ? Brent Chronicle Ra	2
	19th	1.30pm 5 pm	Lumber carting Slab, Shot to Abattoy Bailleul with animal CB 208. L/Cpl. Taylor + then to Schaeskene for Brakes. Pte Roberts to Bailleul Station to meet A.V.C. Sgt. reinforcements for 16th Divl. RSA	1
	20th		Shot black from 11 Railhead for return 5.30am earlier drawing until further notice. (6.30am.) Cpl Taylor to Shot to Abattoir Bailleul with animal CB 236 for Labelon. Lumber carting Slab, 2 pts. to Scherpenberg for Brats & 2 RR's going for Sand, 4 Gals. on all. 10.30 Pte Shepston arrived from 2nd R Bet Suffolks 4/19 and S.O.S. (Mar.3.SM) Pte Winckly Thurston inoculated by M.O. 12 B.S. Eqm	1
	21st	9am 9.45	Shot to LILLEGATE YPRES for animal of 2nd Canadian tunnelling Co. Shot sent first fair. Animal appeared too far removed to RENINGHELST. Sgt. Shot and Cpl. A.V.C. reports Rd. to A.D.V.S. for duty with A.V.B. B.C. of 160 Inf. Bde R.F.A. Sgt. Relieved by order of A.D.V.S. from the men brought by Sgt. Morgan	10. 1st Continued

2nd Continued

Army Form C. 2118.

WAR DIARY (Dec 1916)
or
INTELLIGENCE SUMMARY. 47th Mobile Section A.V.C
16th Division

(Erase heading not required.)

47th MOBILE SECTION, A.V.C.
No. 9
Date 1/1/17

Place	Date	Hour	Summary of Events and Information	Remarks and references to Appendices
NEUTOUTRE	Dec 21 Continued		S/S Spiers returned from leave.	Animals
		1.30 pm	Cpl Taylor + 3 men to Schaeghin for 16 loads timber	
		3 pm	Evacuated on party returned from STOMER	
		6 pm	Capt Smith lectured S/Sgt the 16th Div established on Horse Management time one hour.	
	22nd		Limber & GS load returned. Wagon to Bailleul. Then to Schaeken for 2 loads of timber.	1
		2 pm	S/S B & Crary for 2 loads of gravel. Limbers for coal & rage	
			S/Sgt Langton arrived from 16th Divl Co to act as Leader of rations for A.V.S.	
	23rd	1.30 pm	Cpl Taylor + 3 men to Schaeken for 4 loads of timber limbers & wagon carting stabs, gravel, sand all day	1
	24th		Horses & Leading cleaning, vehicles washed. Animals C13 219 Destroyed & Burned.	3
		3 pm	Wagon to Canada Corral for pump & piping for water troughs Divn Horse to A.S.C. transferred from 112 Fd Ambulance to 10/6 C.O.S. and Drivers Shaw arrived from 142 G.S add to replace.	
	25th Xmas		All morning a general cleaning up of Stable & Camp ground	1
	26th		Cpl Taylor + 4 men for 4 loads bricks from Schaeken. Wagon & limber carting sand and all available men road-making Capt Lawton O/c.	6
	27th	11 am	Limber carting material for road.	1
		1.30 pm	2 Pte to Schaeken for timber	
			1 Cpl + 2 Pte do do	

WAR DIARY or INTELLIGENCE SUMMARY

Army Form C. 2118.

47th MOBILE SECTION, A.V.C.

Dec 1916

47th Mobile Section A.V.C. 16th Division

Place	Date	Hour	Summary of Events and Information	Remarks and references to Appendices
WESTOUTRE	Dec 28th /16		Wagon & Lorries carting material for roads. All available men working on roads. Ophlanta &c. Wagon for coal wood.	Animals Admitted
	Dec 29th	9.30am	Lorries taking 7 animals by barge from Bac St Maur to St Omar. Sgt Mason +3 men O/C on stock cars. Party relieved 5pm. Lorries & Wagon carting bricks for roads. 1 NCO + 12 men to Dranoutre Baths. 2 Pts to Kokeraken for 6 loads of bricks. 2 Pts + RE party for 2 loads of gravel	1
	30th		Sgt Mason returned from leave. Remainder of section to Divisional Baths.	
		11am	2 Pts to Kokeraken for bricks followed at 1.30pm by other 2 Pts. 4 loads in all	
		12.45pm	2 Pts to Bailleul for 1500 bricks. 1 load gravel. Lorries sent to clear commenced clipping section horses with special set machine Clipper Head (Bernard) averages 4 hr 8 mins	2
	31st		Lt Colvin Report made + issued to enable him concentrated format during month of December. 65 gallons petrol.	
		12.45pm	4 Motor Lorries, 3 with gravel, 41 with 1500 bricks. All vehicles washed during morning. Lorries carting bricks all afternoon.	3

Fenton
Capt. A.V.C.
O/C 47th M.S.
A.V.C.

WAR DIARY for month of JANUARY, 1917.

VOLUME 14

H.T. Mobile Vety Section

Vol 13

Army Form C. 2118.

47th MOBILE SECTION, A.V.C.
No. 0504
Date 2/2/17

WAR DIARY
or
INTELLIGENCE SUMMARY January 1917

(Erase heading not required.)

47th Mobile Veterinary Section 16th Div.

Instructions regarding War Diaries and Intelligence Summaries are contained in F. S. Regs., Part II. and the Staff Manual respectively. Title Pages will be prepared in manuscript.

Place	Date	Hour	Summary of Events and Information	Remarks and references to Appendices
WESTOUTRE	Jan 1st/1917		1 Cpl +3 Pts to BAILLEUL for 2 loads gravel. (Motor Lorries) Crane & for motor lorries. 2 Pts to Schaexken for 2 loads old bricks. 2 Pts to R.E. Quarry for 2 loads gravel. Wagon + 4 horses carting road making material on to Section premises.	Appendix attached 8
	2nd Jan.		Float to C.B.10th R.Fd. for animal C.13,262. Limbers wagon carting material for roads all day. 1 Sgt +3 Pts to Schaexken for 4 loads bricks. Float to 9th Corps Cavalry for animal C.13,266	6
	3rd		Limber wagon carting bricks etc for road repairs. 2 Pts to Schaexken. 2 Pts for gravel R.E. Quarry. 2 loads.	3
	4th		Hours altered for parades, owing to heavy road repairs + short daylight. Reveille 6am with intervals of one hour for dinner, Horses out after 9pm. Wagon + Limber carting for road repairs. 1 Sgt + 3 Pts to Schaexken for 4 loads bricks.	4?
	5th		Evacuated 12 animals by road to ST OMER. Sgt Morgan + Cpl Taylor i/c with 16 Drivers of Artillery. 2 Pts to Schaexken for bricks 2 loads. Dismounted duty, Section horses on evacuation are N.S.	3
	6th		3 Pts dismounted to Schaexken for 4 loads bricks. Limber for road tuned. Got Network of stables cleaned, disinfected + limewashed, all Section horses out at work. Pte Hopkins granted leave Jan 7th to Jan 17th. Pte Blackburn returned from leave. Wagon carting for road making all day	3
	7th		Wagon to Canada Corner for building materials to Lorries with tools for repairs. Dfr Martin with Pack Horse to Canada C with water for Piping, replaced with mare for water, trough Limber carting for road making. Animal C.13,266 destroyed. R.H. + Carcase burned	1
	8th		Limber carting material for roads. 2 Pts to Schaexken for 2 loads bricks. Evacuation party returned from ST OMER. 2 Pts for 2 loads gravel. 6pm 2 Pts paraded for inoculation. Capt. Hawton inoculated Second dose Dvr Hogarth evacuated from 112th F.H.Amb. to R.M.Stationary H (Dental Treatment)	4

Army Form C. 2118.

WAR DIARY or INTELLIGENCE SUMMARY

(Erase heading not required.)

No. 47th MOBILE SECTION, A.V.C.

Date 31.2.17

H.Q. Mobile Veterinary Section 16th Div.

Place	Date	Hour	Summary of Events and Information	Remarks and references to Appendices
WESTOUTRE	Jan 9th 1917		Pte Burbage to 142nd A.S.C. as divisional (Cemy?) Farrier Sgt McLeese, Pte Shackburn to bring back horses.	Animals Admitted 1.
			Host collected animal C/3 330 from 142nd A.S.D. 2 Pte to Scheerken for bricks Lumber resting material to Roads. Wagon under repair.	
	10th		Rubber tubing trucks etc. to section premises. Water cart to ordnance for stores. 2 Pte to Scheerken for bricks. 1 Pte to R.S. Quarry for gravel. 1 to do on use. Capt Hesslam, Sgt Morgan, 1 Pte + Driver + limber to HOPOUTRE to destrain and examine 574 remounts	18
	5.30pm		3 Pte paraded at an O's office for inoculation	
	6 pm			
	11th		Evacuated 22 animals by road to STOMER Cpl Godfrey I/c with 5 Animals Sgt Morgan to D.A.C. to collect head collars from remounts. Joined limber party for road repair new part limber under repair. 3 Pte to Scheerken n 4 loads of bricks	6
	12th		Host to D 180th & R.S.C for animal C/3 353. Firepart limber carting bricks etc on to section premises 2 Pte for 2 loads bricks from Scheerken 2 Pte for 2 loads gravel from W.S. Quarry. Pte Barnes granted leave Jan 13th to 23rd. One Pte to stable to bring horses back. 3 Pte paraded a O's office for inoculation	1
	13th		3 Pte to Scheerken for 4 loads bricks. All these brick parties carry bricks to dig out the bricks from the last time abandoned wagons are loaned by Divisional Bakerie. Wagon & Limber repair by civilian wheelwright. Limber to Stores for coal, wood and boot repairs.	
	14th		Evacuation Party 1 Cpl + Pts returned from STOMER. Limber to Ordnance for Stores. Limber + wagon carting bricks on to roads.	31
	15th		Cpl Godfrey + Pte Thos t. to 180th Bde R.F.a. to disinfect stabling (Mange). 2 Pte to Scheerken for 2 loads bricks. 2 Pte to R.S. Quarry for gravel. Evacuated 36 animals by road to St Omer. Sgt Morgan I/c with 1/Bm.m. + 9 Drivers of Artillery	3

Army Form C. 2118.

WAR DIARY
or
INTELLIGENCE SUMMARY

January 1917

47 Mobile Veterinary Section 16th Divn

(Erase heading not required.)

Place	Date	Hour	Summary of Events and Information	Remarks and references to Appendices
WESTOUTRE	Jan 16th/17		3 Pts. to Schachen for 4 loads bricks. Limber Wagon carting bricks to lecture premises. Limber for extra coal for making balcony (drying & washing) suit. Wagon drew 20 Bales of Chaff from dump on Red Steen Cliffs daily issue.	Animals Mounted
	17th		2 Pts. to Schacken for 2 loads bricks. 2 Pts to R.S. Query for 2 loads gravel. Wagon for 15 Bales of Straw from dump to complete issue. Bus to locis for boot repairs. Sgt Morgan & Evacuation Party returned from St Omer.	10
	18th		Evacuated 10 animals to St Omer by road. Sgt Mason & 3 Pte 5/C. Animals taken to 5st Jans Capelles for conveyance to St Omer by motor Ambulance. Pte Manchester & ranked leave Jan 19th to 29th. Pte Stephens returned from Sto Omer. 3 Ptes to Locis for 4 loads bricks. Sgt Morgan & Evacuation Party returned to [premises] as preventative against mange. 11 Horses of section. Rations, evacuation work, washed with calcium.	5
	19th		Evacuated 2 animals by motor Ambulance to St Omer. Limbers to A.S.V.S for Bran. Wire to Canada Corner for coal. work. Limber carting old iron for drainage recovered.	
	20th	9am	Sgt Godfrey & Pte King to Walls of 11 Platoon Batt. to disinfect stables, return 3pm. 3 Pts. to Blaringhem 4 loads shops, owing to hard frost could only get 3 loads. 2 of which had to be left at D.A.C lines and the other unloaded on road dump. Duty completed 7pm.	
		3.30pm	Inspection of section lines & premises by Major General Victor [illeg.].	
	21st		Sgt Mason & Evacuation Party returned from St Omer. Evacuation Party. Riders, clothes etc. hot water calcium. 2 Inspected mange cases clipped out and washed with calcium	1
	22nd	6am	Evacuated 414 animals by road to St Omer. Pt Godfrey & Pte S/3 with 3 Artillery Drivers. Sgt Morgan left for Accident Station en route to 10 Veterinary Hospital & transferred.	245
		8.30	Cho Lucas to 1X Corps Horse dip returned 11 am dip not open.	2
		1.30pm	Wagon to ration dump for additional days hay to reduce road transport in case of thaw. 2 Pts to Schacken for 2 loads bricks, 2 Ptes to R.S. Query for 2 loads gravel.	

WAR DIARY or INTELLIGENCE SUMMARY

Army Form C. 2118.

47th MOBILE SECTION, A.V.C.

Place	Date	Hour	Summary of Events and Information	Remarks and references to Appendices
NESTOUTRE	Jan 23rd/17		Evacuated 9 animals to No 23 Stationary by train from Bde. H.Q. 3 Pts to Schwarzenbor to Casa Bricks. Limber to Isenberche supplied for one days use. To Arthur road transport in case of snow. Bombardt 142 to A.D.C. attd class for 1/4 day. Envy animals of 112 Mobile Ambulance 446 Brandy O.R.S. examined by Capt Easton for Range.	Animals Attended 10 3
	24th		Capt Easton examined all animals of H Bty R.B. for symptoms of mange. 2 Pts to R.E. Rouy for gravel, ramp to front. No wagons available. Wagon carrying team for drainage on road no mange. Stange case clipped out and washed. Limber to ordnance for Stores and A.D.V.S. for Bran. 1 Sgt + 2 Pts paraded from R.O.'s office for inoculation. R.v.O. not present. Pte Brant paraded leaving Jan 24th to Feb 1st.	3
	25th		One Pte to Canada Corner as guide to convoy of wagons with broken limbs for war/repair. Evacuated 10 animals by rail to St Omer. A Eple Gunn + Pte Chapbeer 3/c. Pte Lucas to IX Corps Horse dip to be inslated. Rationed there. Dvr Hogarth A.S.C. returned to duty from R.O. to Stationary Hospital. Pte Brown returned from leave. Sgt Gulfer Vermination party returned from St Omer.	1
	26th		Limber to A.O.V.S. + Stores for 2 Socks Bran. Limber wagon carting bricks to Hoads. 2 Pts to R.E. Bunny for 2 loads gravel. Limber to Lovie for coal. Animal shoot repairs. Capt Easton inspected all animals of St Bon R.B. for symptoms of mange.	1
	27th		3 Horses to Leave for animals C.B. 464 afternoon. Sheet to describe for animal of 112 Field Ambulance. Capt Easton inspected all animal of 112 Field Ambulance.	5
	28th		Pte Blackburn to IX Corps Cavalry returning. Two animals C.B. 462 + 463. Q.M.O. Guess + Pte Chappell returning from St Omer. Inspection of all small tree responses by Capt Easton.	1

Army Form C. 2118.

WAR DIARY
or
INTELLIGENCE SUMMARY

(Erase heading not required.) 47th Mobile Veterinary Section 16th Div

January 1917.

Place	Date	Hour	Summary of Events and Information	Remarks and references to Appendices
WESTOUTRE	29th January		Wagon & Limber carting old tins of Vaseline Premises for cleaning of new roads. Limber to Ordnance for store Lorry for making up Calcs. Sulph. Limber to IX Corps Home Dép for 100 lb Sulphur 30th Rens. 2 Pte. to R.S. Army Headquarters to Orders. Paraded at A.D.O's office for inoculation	Animals Admitted
	30th		Pte. Hopkins to W.O.U.S. Office, discharged duty. Limber to W.O.V.P. for 200 lb Sulphur. Arrangement made to Div. Armourer Shop for overhauling in readiness for disinfection Party	"
	31st	11am	Sgt. Godfrey & 2 Pte. to Stables of B180th & 130th R.S.A. for disinfection Standings. Capt. Renton superintended the carrying out of this work. Returned 3pm. 3 Pte. with 5 Horses to IX Corps Horse Pond. 2 Pte. for 2 loads gravel from R.S. Army 1 Sgt. & 1 Driver paraded at A.D.O's office for inoculation. Wagon to Straw Dump for 1396 lbs of Straw. 203 Gallons of Liq. Calc. Sulph. (concentrated) made & issued during the month.	"

[signature] Renton
Capt. are
O.C. 47th M.V.S

WAR DIARY.

FOR MONTH OF FEBRUARY, 1917.

VOLUME 15

UNIT:- 47th Mobile Veterinary Sectn.

Vol 14

Army Form C. 2118.

WAR DIARY
or
INTELLIGENCE SUMMARY.
(Erase heading not required.)

47th Mobile Veterinary Section
16th Division

February 1917

No. O 696
13/2/17

Place	Date	Hour	Summary of Events and Information	Remarks and references to Appendices
WESTOUTRE	Feb 1st/1917		Wagon further to Canada Corner Farm for coal wood, also for tar for new stables. Cotton drawers sent to Divd Laundry for transmission to Base. Replaced by woollen ones. DRO 2060 24/1/17	Animals Admitted 2
	2nd		Section rodes exercised round the large training ring, owing to severe frost on the ground of thaw. Wagon to N.W.D.L.C. lines for additional days hay and oats with a view to reducing transport or roads in the event of thaw. Other + Drive Hannah sent to 142 CB AVC for refresher 8 animals taken to IX Corps Horse Dip. S/Major + 3 Pts in charge 2 Pts on leave for 2 days. travel from R.E. Quarry	1
	3rd		Other men on private leave to U.K. Sgt + R.S. Wagon to R.E. Quarry for ballast of road. Put mini horses returned from leave. Arleyes. London, Dochestere + Boulogne. All section stables thoroughly disinfected.	1
	4th	10 am	1 Private to Wijtschaete during the coldest heat Collar from Sty Remounts, only completed 3.15 p.m. Wagon to R.E. Quarry for one load of sand. Lorry one load ting from 118th Fd Ambulance. Orderly Quartermaster Sgt IX Corps Horse Dip with letter from DIVS late to ordnance for stores	1
	5th		Wagon to R.E. Quarry for one load sand. Lorry for one half time.	1
	6th		1 G.S. Wagon loads of bricks from R.E. Park, for flooring of new range stable	1
	7th	9 am	Sgt Godfry with three private to P/1/50 M Bde R.F.A. to disinfect standings fittings Capt Linton superintended work. last completed 4.45 p.m. Pte Rice AVC R.O.314 arrived as reinforcement from R. 13 B V Sh Wagon for one load tiro. Capt Tulpin and Irwin went with 12 animals to IX Corps Horse Dip. Capt Linton in the late.	1
	8th		Pts Irwin returned from leave delayed at Boulogne & London. 8th 1007 & 1207 R U S F Port Wagon for two loads of tiros. Block to Bentham to collect animal left with inhabitant	1 W.

2333 Wt. W3314/1454 700,000 5/15 D. D. & L. A.D.S.S./Forms/C. 2118.

Army Form C. 2118.

WAR DIARY
or
INTELLIGENCE SUMMARY.
(Erase heading not required.)

February 1917
47th Mobile Veterinary Section
16th Division

Instructions regarding War Diaries and Intelligence Summaries are contained in F.S. Regs., Part II. and the Staff Manual respectively. Title pages will be prepared in manuscript.

Place	Date	Hour	Summary of Events and Information	Remarks and references to Appendices
WESTOUTRE	Feb 9th 1917		Wagon loads of Bread from R.E. Quarries. 2 Wagon loads of Firewood. Wagon to leave for coal wood	1
	10th		Wagon for 2 loads of firewood. Capt Keaton to Hopoutre re Drafest returns (F. 76.)	2
	11th		Old Crocks with Div Wagon to D.A.C. in L collect 46 Shear Colts from Remounts	5
	12th		2 Loads of firewood from Westoutre, 1 from here. Limber to S.D.M Workshops Bailleul & repair Wagon for Straw, Brown Stone, 14 Sacks 2 Sacks has gone to S.V.H. Mule & orders to 1st Corps Horse Dep with Message from A.D.V.S. Brads with wagon to Westvorleshoek siding returning unserviceable Clothing Stores Ship	1
	13th		Capt Keaton proceeded on Animal C.B. 4.76. Wagon 2 loads of firewood. Limber & Ambulance sent to Rail Head	3
	14th		Promised Orderley to S.D.M. Bailleul with certificate for Limber sent to Railhead & Boot repair to Divisional Boot Shop.	15
	15th		Capt Keaton to El Rue to attend a demonstration or Range at Rs 23 Vet Shop. Evacuated 22 animals by rail to 4 C.V.S. T.D. Dermot, Sgt Bodge, & 2 men o/c Animal C.B.404 Dud, Eruck of Rath Gangrene. Animals annexed Sh.	4
	16th		Drove into town to S.D.M evacuated to Bailleul for Shop (Hawcy late repaired) 1 Road fm from leave. 1 foot snow from here. R.B. & gassy.	1
	17th		Wagon for 1 Road firewood. Reinforcements (incr) passed on ft for duty in compliance with orders Railhead returned from leave to U.K.	1
	18th		3 Horses of 1st Corps Cavalry (cure) spared as ft for duty. In compliance with New instructions vehicle traffic to be reduced to a minimum. Evacuation Party returned from Div Shop	1

2353 Wt. W.2344/1434 750,000 5/15 D.D.&L. A.D.S.S./Forms/C.2118.

Army Form C. 2118.

47th MOBILE SECTION.

No. ....
Date 1/3/17

WAR DIARY February 1917.
or
INTELLIGENCE SUMMARY. 47th Mobile Veterinary Section
16th Division
(Erase heading not required.)

Instructions regarding War Diaries and Intelligence Summaries are contained in F. S. Regs., Part II. and Staff Manual respectively. Title pages will be prepared in manuscript.

Place	Date	Hour	Summary of Events and Information	Remarks and references to Appendices
WESTOUTRE	Feb 19th/1917		Wagon for 2 loads of tins	2
	20th		Capt Gordon to Standings of 11 K Bank to supervise work of disinfection Party. Pg & Sap/py and 3 Privates of 47 MSn DTS	3
	21st		Wagon for one load of tins from St Laurentis. Sgt Godfrey unwell & sent to standings of D/77th Bde to disinfect stabling 1:30pm returned Lty Simpkins 5:45pm	1
	22nd		Wagon made 3 journeys to Wootentin for 3 loads of Zoro for race track. Col Cockshire to R.O.C. Rouen to ad.l. to Reculellas from remount. Sgt Godfrey admitted to hospital 112th Field Ambulance (bronchitis)	4
	23rd	9am	Cpl Taylor & Party disinfected horse standings of D/77 + C/P3 Bdes. returned 3pm Capt Gordon visited horse lines of units under Ml Veterinary Chge and the Supervised work of disinfection party. Wagon for 1 load of tins from Locre and the Ambulance Store	2
	24th	3:30pm	On horseback with horse to Bailleul for float returned at 5pm motor ho. One man 16 IV K Corps Horse Disp with 9 animals returned 5:45pm Wagon for 2 loads of tins Ballaghers to 16 Div G Cs with animal U8492 cured.	1
	25th		Wagon to 7th Corps Horse Disp for time to be used in the making of Sig Cabin. Pulph for treatment (bearing ly) mange cases 11 G1 Sgt Dunlop J. AVC referred Wife of. Denly Y attached 4/7th MVS arriving turnover to a unit of the 16th Div	21
	26th		Cpl Taylor & party to Lingus Camp for disinfect stabling of 176 Co R8. Evacuated 20 animals by road to Lt Omery Sgt Dunlop Eman 3/c. Wagon for one load of tins one load of tins.	5

B.J.

B 353 Wt.W 2544/1454 700000 5/15 D. D. & L. A.D.S.S./Forms/C. 2118.

Army Form C. 2118.

WAR DIARY
or
INTELLIGENCE SUMMARY.

January 1917

(Erase heading not required.)

Instructions regarding War Diaries and Intelligence Summaries are contained in F. S. Regs., Part II. and Staff Manual respectively. Title pages will be prepared in manuscript.

Place	Date	Hour	Summary of Events and Information	Remarks and references to Appendices
WESTOUTRE	Feby 27/17		Wagon carted 5 loads of bricks from road dump to R.E. section forming Wagon to Canada corner. R.E. Cart for water pump.	2
	28th		Wagon to Steen Dump for 15 Bales of straw. 217 Gallons of Lysol Liquoris (Concentrated) issue and issued to units during the month.	1

Newton Capt are
O.C. 47th A.V.S.

WAR DIARY
FOR MONTH OF MARCH, 1917.

VOLUME 16

UNIT:- 4Y? Mobile Vety Section A.V.C.

WAR DIARY or INTELLIGENCE SUMMARY

Army Form C. 2118.

47th Mobile Veterinary Section
15th Division

March 1917

Place	Date	Hour	Summary of Events and Information	Remarks and references to Appendices
METEREN	Feb 1st/1917		Evacuation party returned from St Omer. 1 Sgt & 3 Ptes.	Answers to admin: Posts
		7.0am	OC Septr and 4 Ptes to Vieuxberquin horse standings of A180 and C77 Bdes R.F.A. Duty completed 1.45pm. Capt Benton supervised work.	1
	2nd		Pte Pheasant grazier leave held 3/1/17 to March 13/1/17. Pte Shepston to Bailleul Station to bring saddle horses left. Sgt Dunlop A.V.C. (surplies dressing Sgt.) transferred to C77 A Bde as Act. Cpl. 2 B.S. 100pr loads of bricks & flooring of horse range stable. Ballsign to horse lines for coal exhaust.	"
	3rd		Belthp to Canada Corner to retrieve horse bodies brought back. 2 loads of horses Sicered.	"
	4th		2 animals transferred by mob ambulance to No.3. John H. Stomer Our add to Rothleus for new surgeon lumbered. Party of 4 men for loading and unloading bricks for stable flooring. 2 B.S. Wagons lent by Rural Train.	27
	5th		Evacuated 33 animals to Home lines - 6 Drivers of C/162 Bde R.F.A. and 3 R.F.A. AVC on Substitute Staff wagon to Canada Corner for Vaccines and to Ambulance for litters.	
	6th		Pte Burns reported ADVS office 9am as Leader of Guard line from IX Home Dip. 1 Sgt and 3 Ptes disinfected stables of 142nd ald. Capt Benton supervised work. Duty completed 6.10pm. Wagon to Estaminetvelde for one load of SR Fascines.	1
	7th		1 Surgeon on loan from Home Transport Depot, marked, passed ready for action, listed to H6th Amm Train (Div Waynith 2 Horses). For Journey of Army to proceed to Hazebrouck.	7
	8th		2 Ptes reported at ADVS office for filling sacks with quick lime for manure trench of Divn. Evacuation Party returned from Donier.	4
		5.30pm	Knackerd returned from Steystenuck, wagon duly handed over.	1

Army Form C. 2118.

WAR DIARY
or
INTELLIGENCE SUMMARY 47th Mobile Veterinary Section
(Erase heading not required.)

Army Vet Corps 16th Div.

March 1917

Place	Date	Hour	Summary of Events and Information	Remarks and references to Appendices
WESTOUTRE	Feb 9/1917		Limber to Loere for coal issued.	Animals Admitted
	10th		2 Animals evacuated by Motor Ambulance to 6/23 F.A. Horse. Limber to Ordnance for Stores and to Canada Corner for one load of Drawn Clerks.	7
	11th		One sick horse for E.C Wyn. (employee) loan from 112th Fd Ambulance) Wyn to Canada Corner for three loads from range slats.	36
	12th		2 animals evacuated by Motor Ambulance to St Omer. Limber to Ordnance for stores and to Bundle Corner for three loads. Emergency 35 animals by road to St Omer. Capt Coulter acting A.D.V.S. - Major Andrews on leave.	-
	13th		E.C Wyn with four horses for 3 loads of Timo for road Dranonges (Am Loss)	1
	14th		E.C Wyn with four horses for 2 loads of Vino (Am) from districts and 2 loads for young horse.	1
	15th	am	Float to D.A.C for one horse another journey for mule from Mt A & B & C. Wyn and four horses for one load of which from R Symony Limber to Ordnance for Stores and to Canada Corner for one load of drawn clerks. Emergency party returned from St Omer.	2
	16th		Float and two horses for animal from A 180th Bdes. Eleven four horses for one load stabs. All these returned from leave. Float to C 77th A.S.a Bde for sick animal. Limber to Loere for coal issued.	30
	17th		E.F Wagon and four horses Carting School Stn. for road damp to stables. Float for animal of C180th Bde. Limber to Loere for coal issued for old tins.	12

2449. Wt. W14957/Mg0 750,000 1/16 J.B.C. & A. Forms/C.2118/12.

Army Form C. 2118.

WAR DIARY or INTELLIGENCE SUMMARY
(Erase heading not required.)

47th Mobile Section A.V.C.
A.D.V.S.
16th Division
1917

Place	Date	Hour	Summary of Events and Information	Remarks and references to Appendices
WESTOUTRE	Nov 18th/1917		Float and 2 horses to D/177 for animal. Finished for 2 loads of timber.	advanced
	19th		Wagon & 4 horses for slabs. Sent for 2 loads timber. Limber to Ordnance for stores.	2
	20th		Wagon & 4 horses for 2 loads of timber. Animal C.13.635 Ansa was returned to Bureau. Capt Scott attended A.D.V.S. conference.	
	21st		Wagon & 4 horses for 2 loads of timber from Bulscheute. Animal C.13.622 Destroyed returned and buried. Specimen + Chloroform Sent.	
	22nd		Wagon & 4 horses for 2 loads timber from Locre.	4
	23rd		Mule C.13 was taken in float to Bulscheute at Bailleul. Wagon for 1 load of timber. Limber for coal issued from Locre.	1
	24th		Wagon & 4 horses for 2 loads of timber from Locre	2
	25th		Float & 5 horses to D/177 A52 Base to bring animal to A.V. Wagon Lines.	
	26th	9 am	Evacuating party 1 Sgt & Pte I.C. Pte H.B. St Omer by train with sick animals. Capt Lewis and Lt Speller to new area to arrange for camp etc. & billets. Opl. & Men from camp, fatigue work. E.L Wagon & 4 horses took 2 loads of camp material billets. Limber to Locre for one load old iron.	5
	27th		Capt Scott and Interpreter made final arrangements to leave camp. Opl Taylor & Men working at their camp. E.L Wagon & horses took 2 loads of material Limber carting road Rubble and stone from Locre 8.30am to 5pm	

WAR DIARY or INTELLIGENCE SUMMARY

Army Form C. 2118.

47th Mobile Veterinary Section
16th Div.
March 1917

Place	Date	Hour	Summary of Events and Information	Remarks and references to Appendices
WESTPUTRE	March 28th 1917	11am	E.I.W 75pr. 7 horses to new camp with 1 head mallein. Cpl Taylor 2 men making preps. E.I.W 75pr. 22 horses brought in with unserviceable shoes. Casualty 916 returned 5.30pm. Buyer & driver returned from leave. Capt Stanton finishes duty as acting A.D.V.S.	Annexe "STRENGTHS" 4
	29th		E.I.W 75pr. 12 horses to Watou Stn. 2 RFA to remake tyres wagon. Wagon returned. Brought 112 H. & H. Out Horse and 2 horses to collect remount of B/109 Fld. OSA. Capt Stanton to inspect animals horses to strain dump.	2
		9pm	Evacuation Party returned from St. Omer Capt Smiles mallein'd estimated of B. Corps Cavalry.	
	30th	9.30am	Cpl. Taylor & 5 men to Boege at Brogenmark with animals for R23 VH. Returned at 3.30pm Lt. (?) B.E. disinfected time & bedding of M3 Fld. Ambulance Lankus 45 horses to new dump. 6 men to trade of stores, Ops. Evts. In Sinsen for evac. wound (Sinson)	5
		8pm	Horse to loves to dump for 1 load of stores. (loves) Capt Smiles mallein'd 32 animals "H.B." Corps Cavalry.	
	31st	7.30am	Horses to horses to office of A.D.V.S. for remainder of office equipment. Evacuation returned at 6. Section with all veterinary stores. E.I.W Sinsage. E.I.W 75 NTS new camp with mallein personnel, making. Cpl. Taylor 45 men at work there. O.C. & Personnel of 31st M.V.S. arrived, acting under instructions from O. 19th Div. to take over section in presence of A.H. 7th 16th D.I.S. 236 Sections of Lup Allso Lucps (Brown dates) horses and harness returned to work during March	5

W. Kennetts Capt. A.V.C.
O.C. 47th M.V.S.

WAR DIARY FOR MONTH OF APRIL, 1917.

VOLUME:- 17

UNIT:- No. 4 Mobile Vet. Section A.V.C.

Army Form C. 2118.

WAR DIARY
or
INTELLIGENCE SUMMARY.
(Erase heading not required.)

April 1917

47th MOBILE SECTION, A.V.C. 09/19
Date 1/5/17

Place	Date	Hour	Summary of Events and Information	Remarks and references to Appendices
WESTOUTRE	1/4/17		Rides to New Site with Horses. Retired Stores. Horses returned to Base. Full loads of old tins for remaking to new premises. Lorries also got one load of tins. O.C. & Personnel of 31st R.I.J. left for a Temp: Camp.	Animals Admitted 15
	2nd		Horses 1, 2 Horses to Rozelles DAC for animal CB 711. Lorries to transit stores of old tins. Patients with sick horses taken to relieve for stores.	
		3.30pm	Hors't 1 & 2 horses to 513 the DAC for animal CB 7115, taken direct to Wipers Lorry. Horst returned 9.45pm. 1 Pte sent on Cycle acting ready for evacuations tomorrow.	5
	3rd	8.30am	2 horses & van to leave for S.A. Wagon on empty train. also loaded 22 Guernsies for road to new site.	
		9 am	Lorries took 19 animals from Section T and 21 if Actual C.Os from Wippenhock Acting Party of 1 R.C.D. 16 men for evacuating animals. Lorries to Kreve to draw Kneed Cake for sick animals. Horse Wagon for 1 horse two each. Lorries to IX th Corps Horse O/b with 22 hides for conveyance to Base. Animals CB 8.00 659 4701 Destroyed, Skinned & Buried	1
	4th	6.30am	Horst 2 horses to Kop 100 C.C.U. for animal CB 2.716 returned 12 noon. Major 4 horses to Kreve for 3 loads of Tins for new road.	1

Army Form C. 2118.

WAR DIARY
or
INTELLIGENCE SUMMARY.

(Erase heading not required.)

47th MOBILE SECTION, A.V.C.
No. 9/19
Date 15/1/17

Instructions regarding War Diaries and Intelligence Summaries are contained in F.S. Regs., Part II. and the Staff Manual respectively. Title page will be prepared in manuscript.

April 1917.

Place	Date	Hour	Summary of Events and Information	Remarks and references to Appendices
Westoutre	5/4/17		Wagon & Lorries for 3 loads of Twin for new site (Ordnance Ry) Also 2 Horses to C/100 RGA for annual CB732	Animals admitted 16
	6th		Evacuated 20 animals by barge from Base St Maur. Party of 1 RCD + 6 Pte 2 Pte to travel with animals to Base. Lories for 3 loads of Twin taken on trek premises. Wagon 2 loads of Twin + 1 of material. Lories to Locre for coal. Horses. Evacuation Party of 1 RCO + 6 Pte returned from Base.	4
	7th		Wagon to RE Dump for load of building material, also two loads of Twin from Locre. Lories for 2 loads of Twin.	3
	8th		Wagon 1 load Twin. Lories 1 load material to new site. Barge Evacuation Party (2 Pte) returned from Base	1
	9th		Wagon for 2 loads material for new camp. Lories with Mules to Army Park, for transport to Base. Good Pair to collect animals CB743 from Ordnance. veldt. Capt Newton for Government left with animal. Lories to Locre for new Issued Cake. Animals Evacuated by road to 21 Mou: Vy Party of 1 RCO + 3 Pte	2

WAR DIARY or INTELLIGENCE SUMMARY

Army Form C. 2118.

47th MOBILE SECTION, A.V.C.
No. 9119 Date 1/5/17

April 1917

Place	Date	Hour	Summary of Events and Information	Remarks and references to Appendices
WESTOUTRE	10/4/17		Wagon, Lumber for 1 load lime & 1 load of gravel each for metalling	Animals Admitted
			to new camp. Started horses to Canada Crns Jnr. 1 load Grain	6
		noon	1 RCO & 4 Ors. with Hammels Orange cases to WD Hosp. Horse Dep.	
	11th		2 Wagon for SD Parcels & 1 load of lime. Limber for 2 loads of lime	2
	12th		Wagon for 2 loads of gravel & 1 of lime. Limber for 1 load of gravel	
			Party of time. Limber to Stores depot here for A. [?] time for Remt of Division	14
	13th	11.30am	Party of 1 RCO & 3 Ptes. (Board evacuation Party) returned from base	
			Party of 1 RCO & 2 Ptes with Hammels for evacuation by barge from	
			ESTAIRES. Party returned 4.30 pm	2
			Wagon for 1 load of lime & 1 of gravel. Limber for 1 load/two bales for	
			Coal wood from home.	
	14th		Wagon for 1 load material & 1 of two for R. W. Camp. Limber for 1	9
			load of time & 1 of gravel	
	15th		Wagon for 1 load material for new camp	37
			Limber to Railhead for forage on indent for extra horses in [?]	

47th MOBILE SECTION A.V.C.

Army Form C. 2118.

WAR DIARY
or
INTELLIGENCE SUMMARY.

April 1917.

Place	Date	Hour	Summary of Events and Information	Remarks and references to Appendices
WESTOUTRE 2.H.Q.	16/4/17		Evacuated 52 animals by road to Thenen. Party of 1 N.C.O., 5 Pte. & 5 Dvrs. of 113rd A.St.Road. Wagon for 1 load of timber & 1 P & 1 gravel for road to new Camp. Limbers for 1 load of timber. Stretchbearers to A/177th Bde. Annual C.B. S.O. 816.	Animals Admitted 3
	17th		Wagon for 1 load material from R.E. Dump & 2 loads of timber. Limber for 1 load gravel & 1 load of timber.	6
	18th		Limbers for 1 load timber & 1 of gravel. Wagon for 2 loads of timber. Float to Rouen for repairs to brake, later for 1 load of straw. 1 N.C.O. & 5 Pte. with 10 animals (charge cases) to IX Corps Horse Depot	8
	19th		Wagon for 2 loads of timber for road from present Camp to main road. Rubs. four horses, also got one free load of gravel, same road. Evacuation Party of the 16th and returned from Rane.	9
	20th		Evacuated 12 animals by barge from Cne. Dranov. 1 N.C.O. & 2 Pte. as travelling party also 2 Pte. to answer shipping float & horses to convey one animal to Barge. Wagon for 1 load of timber. Lates for fuel from same.	2

[signature]

Army Form C. 2118.

WAR DIARY
or
INTELLIGENCE SUMMARY.
(Erase heading not required.)

April 1917

47th Mobile Section A.V.C. 9/19 15/17

Place	Date	Hour	Summary of Events and Information	Remarks and references to Appendices
WESTOUTRE 9.h.S.1	21/4/17	9 am	3 Pte with horses saddlery equipment left to join IX Corps A.V.D. Capt Newton with party to hand over	Animals Admitted
			Wgn for 2 loads of timber for wallmaking (Re-enf Camp)	—
	22"		Wgn to R & amb for material for tent camp Animal ABh° 732 Rodriguez Skinned & Buried	27
	23"	Sunday	Evacuation Conducting Party of the 20th returned from Base. Evacuated 49 animals by rail to St Omer. Conducting party of 1 A.C.O. 4 Ohrs & 4 Ors of IX Corps A.V.D. with horse saddlery equipment 1 Sgt of 47th M.T. Proct Capt Newton to hand over Lunches for one load of straw. Capt Newton endeavoured to arrange with contractor for a paddock, also to force to camp a pretend asking if a canvas water tank to Re-Inf Cent Lumber Capt Newton & Tarpn) to the Beam Stores by civilian	1
	24th		Wgn to Knox to 9 O.M. with 1st part timber for repair (broken axle) Capt Layton to impress urgent repair or replacement Wagon for 2 loads timber. Float to 1426 asc Grammer ABh 867.	1

WAR DIARY or INTELLIGENCE SUMMARY

Army Form C. 2118.

April 1917.

Place	Date	Hour	Summary of Events and Information	Remarks and references to Appendices
WEST OUTRE In the field	25/4/17		One workshop & stores for limber repaired at D.M. workshop Ballieul. also brought back news of S. Wagon repairs.	Animals actual strength
	26th		Wagon lumber 2 loads each trip. 1 full load of timber for roadmaking. Limber to Ordnance for stores & to Armourers Shop for fittings to be designed and attached to canvas water tanks.	14.
	27th		Wagon float for 1 load of two. 1 load of two (no. 23) and Limber Wagon for 1 load of two returned. Road conducting party 12 Animals evacuated to Base by barge from Bac St Maur including one flat cast. Lorries for one load of gravel, lakes to Loire for fuel.	—
	28th		Wagon to R.S. Dump for material for new camp. Lorries for one load of two, lumber for 1 load of gravel. 1 of two.	1
	29th		Limber wagon & float washed & oiled. Draught harness thoroughly overhauled & cleaned. Draught horses rested.	24.

B.

Army Form C. 2118.

47th MOBILE SECTION A.V.C.

No. 9/19
Date 1/5/17

WAR DIARY
or
INTELLIGENCE SUMMARY.
(Erase heading not required.)

April 1917

Place	Date	Hour	Summary of Events and Information	Remarks and references to Appendices
WESTOUTRE Int Field	30/4th		Evacuated 25 animals by road to ST OMER. 1 R.C.O. 3 P.S. + admitted 3 駒n of Artillery as Conducting Party. Wagon for 2 Wks of Sept for veterinary to next camp. Float to Ordnance with van to stores for return to O.O Base 2. 70 Gallons of Dip Calvo, Disph. (Concentrated) made and issued during the month.	Animals Admitted
			211 animals admitted during the month. 20 Treated and Returned to Units 3 Destroyed 6 Remaining Under Treatment Remainder evacuated to Base Hospital	

Sewton
Capt.
O.C. 47th A.V.S.

WAR DIARY:
------oOo------

VOLUME:- 18

FOR MONTH OF MAY, 1917.

UNIT:- 4th Mobile Vety Section

Army Form C. 2118.

WAR DIARY or INTELLIGENCE SUMMARY.

(Erase heading not required.)

#7 Mobile Veterinary Section. 16th Div

4TH MOBILE SECTION. A.V.C.
No. O/209
Date. 2/6/17.

May 1917

Place	Date	Hour	Summary of Events and Information	Remarks and references to Appendices
				Animals
WESTOUTRE	May 1st/1917		Limber Wagon 3 loads each of stores material to new camp.	Admitted
			Horse to Frontier post (two journeys) with animals O.B. No 816 and 867 for conveyance to Base by Motor Ambulance.	—
ST JANS CAPPEL 2nd			Pte Shepston to A.D.M.S. for Medical Examination	
			Section moved from M.15.d.7.3. to M.26.b.8.8. Sheet 28.	2
	3rd		Pte Shepston admitted to 71st Field Ambulance. Wagon to Palinge dump with unserviceable stores. Limber to Ordnance with blankets withdrawals, also drew horse shoes &c. Evacuation road Party returned from St Omer.	1
	4th		Limber for coal wood. Gaspart limber with canvas wire tank (designed by Capt Fenton) to water station	1
	5th		Inspection stores with Pkt Helmets, Goggles & Box Respirators	6
	6th		Capt Fenton to 71/2 & 3rd Ambulance LA CLYTE to collect animals wounded by shelfire also to WESTOUTRE to attend wounded animals of same unit. 8 H.D. horses & 1 D mule killed 9 animals wounded. Also collected 3 of these from LA CLYTE. 1 Pte to LA CLYTE to skin carcase of one of the animals killed. Blew tails off 7 others	9

Army Form C. 2118.

WAR DIARY
or
INTELLIGENCE SUMMARY.

May 1917

47th Mobile Veterinary Section 16th Div

Place	Date	Hour	Summary of Events and Information	Remarks and references to Appendices
ST JANS CAPPEL	May 7/1917		Evacuated 4 Animals (Sheel wounds) per Motor Ambulance. Shot to Bone for animal CB 933. Evacuated to Stores by road, 13 animals, 1 RCA. 3 men in charge. Limbered to Ottawa with Winter withdrawals for stores.	Animals Admitted 8
	8th		Evacuated one animal per Motor Ambulance.	2
	9th		Wagon to R.E. Park for material for buildings. Evacuated 2 animals per Motor Ambulance.	5
	10th		Limber to Haegedoorne asking for road material. Road evacuation party returned from STOMER. Wagon limber to HAEGEDOORNE Clay for 3 loads each of material for road. Fleet to La CLYTTE for animal CB 947.	5
	11th		Evacuation 5 animals by hoof from BAC ST MAUR to STOMER. 1 RCO 2 men as conducting party. Wagon drew one load Limber 2 loads of material for road. Wagon to LOCRE for coal wood for advance stores. Limber to IX Corps Dep for Lime.	5
	12th		Evacuated 2 animals per Motor Ambulance to STOMER. Hat B D/180th Bde RFA for animal COL 953. Wagon Limber drew two loads each of material for road. The Private granted 10 days leave to U.K.	2 15/5

WAR DIARY or INTELLIGENCE SUMMARY

Army Form C. 2118.

May 1917
#7th Mobile Veterinary Section 16th Div

Place	Date	Hour	Summary of Events and Information	Remarks and references to Appendices
ST JANS CAPPEL	May 13th 1917	9.4.	Animals C/5 & 9/3 taken in float to abattoir BAILLEUL destroyed by Sgt Mason	Animals Admitted 3
	14th		11 Animals evacuated by road to St OMER one R.E.O. two men 3/C. Barge conducting party of 11 inct. 1 R.E.O. when returned. Demonstration by Capt Benton to personnel of Section and all Sgts A.V.C. of division on method of adjusting Anti Gas Helmet Horse, with & without the evening of the small box Respirator.	1
			Shot to Canada Cross for straw	4
			G.S. Wagon washed and oiled ready for return to unit	
	15th		Shot to LOCRE for Animal C/3 K°. 9/5/8. 2 animals evacuated by Motor Ambulance. G.S. Wagon (on 2 days leave) returned to 113th Stella Ambulance. Shot collected 3 animals. 1 from C/113 R.S.A. Bde & from H & L.a. S.A.C.	2
	16th		Capt Benton granted 14 days leave to U.K. Lieut Cawthorn A.V.C. arrived to take charge of Section? Animal C/131 960 taken to Abattoir BAILLEUL on float and destroyed by Sgt Mason.	1 B.1.
	17th		Shot to Canada Cross for no load of straw	
	18th		Evacuated 9 animals. 1 Stoet Cars by barge. 1 R.E.O. + 2 men to Rouge hides for 1 load material for yard. 2 to 2 for coal +wood. Animal C/13959 destroyed +buried	2

Army Form C. 2118.

WAR DIARY
or
INTELLIGENCE SUMMARY

(Erase heading not required.)

#7 Mobile Veterinary Section 76th Div

May 1917

Place	Date	Hour	Summary of Events and Information	Remarks and references to Appendices
ST JANS CAPPEL	May 19th 17		Rides to Ordnance for stores.	Animals Admitted
			Rides to Abattoir BAILLEUL and destroyed 1 RCD taken with 5 animals (Mange Cases) to IX Corps Horse Dip.	12
	20th		Ride to Ordnance for old canvas for roofing of shed for Mange animals. Float to LOC.R.E. for animals CBSh.924. Rides to AMV Reste & CBSh.905.	8
	21st		Evacuated 11 animals by road to ST OMER. 1 RCD taken S/C. (6 Mange Cases) Staff Sgt Mason (on promotion) transferred to No 13 Veterinary Hospital.	1
	22nd		Rides to Canada Cross Rds for Rats and to Ordnance for stores. One OR granted 10 days leave to U.K.	1
	23rd		Float to C/110th RGA for animal CBSh.906. Rides to DAC regarding for 139 head collars from remounts. Float for one load of straw. Rides for building material for Mange shed. 3 animals Mange Cases taken to IX Corps Horse dip. One OR returned from leave.	2
	24th		Rides to IX Corps Dip for 10 cart horse. Float to CC for straw. Evacuation party returned from ST OMER, the returning horses fed through here en route journey.	3

Army Form C. 2118.

WAR DIARY
or
INTELLIGENCE SUMMARY.
(Erase heading not required.)

47th MOBILE SECTION
No. 9
Date 2/6/17

May 1917
#7 Mobile Veterinary Section 16th Div

Place	Date	Hour	Summary of Events and Information	Remarks and references to Appendices
ST JANS CAPPEL	May 25/17		Duties to Ordnance for Stores. Late for coal & goods. Evacuated 3 animals by barge 1 RD & 1 man 3/c.	Animals Admitted 9
	26th		Duties for evacuations. Start 4 men to LOCRE for 1 load building material. 1 RD & 1 man 3/c.	9
	27th		Start for no load parts.	24
	28th		17 animals evacuated by road to ST OMER 1 RCD & 3 men 3/c. Duties to Ordnance for stores. Interpreter made arrangements for lease of a field for animals (debility cases), fences put up. Start to Watton BAILLEUL with animal ER3.10 9be destroyed by Lt Saylor.	9
	29th		All debilitated animals turned out to graze, in field near camp. Another field leased (near LOCRE) for turning out any debilitated animals of division. Duties with all picketing & feeding equipment also forage to LOCRE, left horse paddock. One pack of section in charge of NCO. Inspection of M.V. carts by branch officer with DDVS. ADVS 16th A.D. S.36th Duties to LOCRE 1 from C/177 1 RSA from 144th CFA. Start collected 3 animals 1 from C/177 R.F.A. & 1/2 ton linseed cake One RO returned as reinforcement from Army Veterinary Hospital	8

Army Form C. 2118.

WAR DIARY
or
INTELLIGENCE SUMMARY.
(Erase heading not required.)

May 1917   47th Mobile Veterinary Section 16th Div

Place	Date	Hour	Summary of Events and Information	Remarks and references to Appendices
ST JANS CAPPELL	May 30th	11	Evacuated 2 animals by Motor Ambulance Hunter to H.Q. Div Train (for active forage Supplementary Indent) Hunter to LOCRE Paddock with forage for 25 animals Sent 15 IX Corps Ordnance Workshop to repair	Annual Return 27
	31st		Hunter to LOCRE Paddock with forage, also took Lieut Cawthorn Kit to rear billet. Capt Lowton returned from leave. 2 Pts from IX Corps M.V.S. arrived for temporary duty Road reconnaissance Party returned from ST OMER	2
		110	Gallons of Liq. Calcic Sulph Concentrate (Mange Dressing) made and issued during the month. Most animals admitted during the month 164 Most Cured and Returned ———— 20 Died or Destroyed ———— 5 Evacuated ———— 69 Remaining Under Treatment ———— 70	

D. ? Linton
Capt
O.C. 47th M.V.S.
16th Div

WAR DIARY.

FOR MONTH OF JUNE, 1917.

VOLUME:- 19

UNIT:- 47/8 Mobile Veterinary Section A.V.C.

WAR DIARY or INTELLIGENCE SUMMARY

Army Form C. 2118.

47th Mobile Veterinary Section
16th Division

June 1917

Place	Date	Hour	Summary of Events and Information	Remarks and references to Appendices
ST JANS CAPPEL M.26.B.8.	June 1st 1917		Limber to Paddock loose with forage and to Ordnance for stores	Animals Admitted
	2nd	9.30	Gun Rifle Inspection and Drill one hour.	2
	3rd		Limber taken to LOCRE Paddock to clean all manure etc. and bring back forage and stores, all horses returned to work, paddock to remain for camp. One private returned from leave.	5
	4th		Evacuated 6 animals by road to ST OMER horse Ambulance.	3
			Limber for 8 bales of chaff from dump. Capt Chappell to A.D.V.S. as [?].	
	5th		Shoot prepared, Called for at IX Corps D.M. later collected animal no. 177 RFA and one from A/156 Bde RFA. Evacuated 2 animals per horse Ambulance	4
	6th		Limber and Drew cleaning up all manure in paddocks, later to IX Corps HQ re disp[?] for sent time. Stock collected 2 animals CB No 96 and 98. One private with Pack horse met saddle to LOCRE for Rd of Dr Smith attached to Section in place of Capt Chappell. (AD/V/S [?]) Pte Horton as orderly to ADVS	10
	7th		Limber to ADVS offices with Lieut. Lineaa Linseed oil, and Gentian for stores. 1 NCO taken to Horse disp with 5" range cases No 7 and [?]	13
			late to dump for Green forage. 2 Off IX Corps ADVD Jemy daily with 47th VS returned to unit	W.

Army Form C. 2118.

WAR DIARY JUNE/1917
INTELLIGENCE SUMMARY. 47 Mobile Veterinary Section
16th Div

(Erase heading not required.)

Place	Date	Hour	Summary of Events and Information	Remarks and references to Appendices
ST JANS CAPPELL M.D. B.E.F.	June 8th 1917		One animal evacuated for motor ambulance. Mules to dump for forage.	Animals Admitted 5
	9th		Capt Carter Lieut Cawthorn 1 NCO 2 Pte. + Pvr with float and pair to KEMMEL for duty at 197th M.V.S. advanced collecting station. Mules for coal removed. OC Section relieved from ADVS duty on orderly completed.	6
	10th		Pte Rice to ADVS with section orders W.S. on empty lorry. Pte Palmer and Dvr Roberts to WESTOUTRE for civilian float on 2d pty tram. Evacuated 30 animals to IX Corps M.V.S. (6 mules float) float returned to rear lorry same evening.	10
	11th		3 horses 4 mules taken to KEMMEL paddock for grazing. Stock brought in animal from advanced station use personal required section mules collected stores & kit except one pte left in charge.	16
	12th		All walking cases + 2 float cases brought in from KEMMEL, mules cleaned up all stores.	3
	13th		Float to Kemmel for one animal. The pte left the required section. Evacuated 33 animals to IX Corps M.V.D. Section moved from M.2.6.B.8.8. to MERRIS F.7.B.3.7. One pte left behind i/c of 8 sick animals in paddock.	1

B.W.

WAR DIARY or INTELLIGENCE SUMMARY

Army Form C. 2118.

JUNE 1917 47th Mobile Veterinary Section 16th Division

Place	Date	Hour	Summary of Events and Information	Remarks and references to Appendices
MERRIS F.9.B.3.7.				Animals Admitted
	June 14th/1917		Wagon to dieadump for forage and stores.	—
	15th		Kit inspection for Exchanges. One pte to WHH 48th Inf Bde. Infantry on draw.	1
	16th		All Saddlery, Harness, Vehicles cleaned up. Evacuated 12 animals (on foot) to No 5 Infm to VS	11
	17th		Section returned to No. 26. B.8.8. Capt Lawton to 112th Field Ambulance. Capt Cawthorn to take command of Section	1
	18th		Section returned to MERRIS F.9.B.3.7. Surplus forage stores left in charge of one NCO.	1
	19th		Capt Cawthorn and OC Section with [?] to farm between STRAZEELE & PRADEELES & collect animal of 113th Field Ambulance. Evacuated, common tone, destroyed, inhabitant to bury Carcase. Old Rice Lithofare horse saddles to IX Corps Horse Dep for Pte Lucas. (to remount station) Rules to salvage with unserviceable clothing and surplus stores. 1 NCO and 4 men of 47th Inf Inf Bde returned to their respective units. OC Surtees returned from WH 48th Inf Bde duty completed. 1 Sgt 3 men withdrawn on detachment duty with 1X Corps M V R rejoined Section.	5
	20th		Evacuated 3 animals (on foot) to N°5 Vet Horse Hosp BORRE. Section moved to GODEWAERSVELDE Q.6.C.77.	1

Army Form C. 2118.

WAR DIARY or INTELLIGENCE SUMMARY.

(Erase heading not required.)

47th Mobile Veterinary Section 16th Div

Instructions regarding War Diaries and Intelligence Summaries are contained in F.S. Regs., Part II. and the Staff Manual respectively. Title pages will be prepared in manuscript.

Place	Date	Hour	Summary of Events and Information	Remarks and references to Appendices
OUDEZEELE O.C.?	June 22nd 1917		Capt Paston (and Pte Case servant) returned from C.C.S. Stock collected during arrival OBR 172 from 144 Coy ASC at EECKE, taken on to X Corps N.V.D. for evacuation. BOESCHEPE, also mule OBR 171.	Animals Admitted 1
	June 22nd/17 23rd		Section moved to ZEGERS CAPPELL. 7.30am arrived 4 p.m. Section moved to B.19 & 6.6. PONT D'ERKELSBRUGGE.	2
	24th		All harness Cavalry wagons cleaned up.	
	25th		Short to BOLLEZEELE for animal OBR 176.	
	26th		Capt Paston to LEDRINGHEM to take Reserve Park Mules for coal. Capt Paston attended who case of Detach of Army Horse A and C Vet Inspector. All supplies withdrawn deficiencies and exchanges noted.	15
	27th		Evacuated 15 animals infirmed to D.M.V., including 1 foot case. Capt Paston 1 R.C.D. to here S/c. Mules to Oudezeele for stores. Capt Paston returned from D.M.V. 8.30pm. remainder of party with feed to follow. Animal OBR 176 (Pneumonia case) Died.	2
	28th		1 R.C.D. party returned from D.M.V.	3

Army Form C. 2118.

WAR DIARY
or
INTELLIGENCE SUMMARY.   #7 Mobile Veterinary Section

(Erase heading not required.)   JUNE 1917

Place	Date	Hour	Summary of Events and Information	Remarks and references to Appendices
Pont Derrelsbauque B.19.a.6.6	June 29/1917		Hont Lt. 113th Field Ambulance for animal CB to 197	Animals admitted 2
	30		Ote Roberts 6th R.I.R. attached to 47th M.V. granted leave to U.K. July 1st to 10th	
			Rides to Ordnance for stores	
			Ote Furlong to H.Q. ord Room. 3 day duty as dresser	
			Animals Admitted 126	
			Cures and Issued 50	
			Aged and Destroyed 2	
			Evacuated 106	
			60 Gallons of Mg (Alia Sulph (Concentrated) made and issued during the month for treatment of mange cases	

W Fenton
Capt
O.C. 47 MVS

WAR DIARY.

FOR MONTH OF JULY, 1917.

VOLUME :- 20

UNIT :- 4 y/F Mobile Veterinary Section
AV&

WAR DIARY or INTELLIGENCE SUMMARY

Army Form C. 2118.

47 Mobile Section A.V.C.
16 K Div.
July 1917

Place	Date	Hour	Summary of Events and Information	Remarks and references to Appendices
BOLLEZEELE B19.a.6.6.	July 1/1917		Capt Fenton, Acting A.D.V.S. pending arrival of D.A.D.V.S.	Animals Admitted — 1
	2nd		Capt Fenton returned to Duties? P/c Chappell to h° 23 V.A. with A.D.V.S.'s horse	1
	3rd		Animal C.B.h° 179 returned to 10 K.R. Dublin Fus. (Age Blackburn)	1
	4th		Capt Fenton visited all units of 47th Inf Bde inspecting animals. Bathing Parade 4 pm to 6.30 pm	1
	5th		Cpl Rineburn on guide for D.A.D.V.S. proceeding to Ameke Station. Ship bush horse.	—
	6th		Lunches with Dunsmith A.D.C. and Pte to D.A.D.V.S. also brought back spare harness &c.	5
	7th		Capt Fenton and Pte Lucas to Bollezeele to hold post mortem on a cow belonging to civilian area, disposed forearm (is desire claim), Lucks to Ordnance for stores. Evacuated 9 animals (1 in float) to h° 23 Hospital St Omer. 1 Cpl 16 men S/c (Evac. 9)	1
	8th		Evacuation Party returned from St Omer. Float to Ameke for C.B.h° 205	1
	9th		Lunches to dump for coal. Capt Fenton to Bollezeele & Volkerinckove visiting Transport lines of 147 A.T.C. 221 A.T.C. R.E.	1
	10th		Wagon to Ordnance for stores. 3pm Inspection of A.V.C. P.6. by D.A.D.V.S.	1
	11th		Shot B.Rabrech Tp Animal C.B. 206. Inspection and instruction for attaching extension to small box respirator, also inspection of P.H. Helmets, by R.S.O. from Divl Gas School	1

WAR DIARY or INTELLIGENCE SUMMARY

Army Form C. 2118.

47th Mobile Veterinary Section 16th Division

July 1917

Place	Date	Hour	Summary of Events and Information	Remarks and references to Appendices
BOLLEZEELE	July 12th 1917	7am	Capt Carlos went out to collect animal left at ambulance farm. Owner went to Signalling Station. Called at ambulance on return for Orders.	Animals Admitted — 1
			No. 724 Staff/Sgt Pickerance S. arrived from No. 2 Vet Hosp. to complete establishment. Section training parade 11am to 12 noon	
	13th		Horse sick few with CBDh 206 to No 23 VMR Bhses. L/Cpl Blackburn f/c. Animal CBDh 207 Destroyed skinned & buried.	1 (Gunner)
			Capt Carlos inspected animals of 155th & 155th Bdes C.R.E. at Herzeleghem.	
	14th		Capt Carlos inspected animals of 112th Fd Ambulance at Rubrouck and 147 AT Co at Arneke	2
			Animal admitted from XIV Corps School for treatment (colic) died later CBDh 210.	
	15th		Animal CBDh 210 skinned & buried	—
	16th		Pte Grant with Sgt Sayers to Tatinghem to bring back horse on loan. Sgt Sayers horse lame. Admitted Section. Capt Carlos inspected animals of 148th Inf/My Bde at Eringhem. Pte Barnes King	3
	17th		Pte Durhinger rejoined Section. Empty duty with 140 TC RSC (horse transport) to Wippenhoek to join 2nd Corps R.V.D. Fully equipped horses transport. Capt Carlos examined animals of 2nd Dublins 47th R Dubfs.	1
	18th		Cpl Hopkins Pte Trenchinston to Wippenhoek to join 2nd Corps R.V.D. Fully equipped horses (Artillery)	
	10.24pm		Message received, animal of 8th R Dublin Guards, broken fetlock. Staff/Sgt Destroyed. Capt Carlos inspected animals of 148th Ambulance Co, 8th Dublins 145 Co ASC. 4111 Field Ambulance.	—

WAR DIARY or INTELLIGENCE SUMMARY

4⁷ᵗʰ Mobile Section AVC 16ᵗʰ Div July 1917

Army Form C. 2118.

Place	Date	Hour	Summary of Events and Information	Remarks and references to Appendices
BOLLEZEELE	July 19.1917	7am	Capt Parker to Wormhoudt to arrange collection of animals left with inhabitant. Short M.2 Pte Gt Taylor 2/c to field carcass of 3 animals killed by train and bury the animal mentioned above. Party returned 3-30 pm. Capt Parker to DADVS Conference. Inoculated animals of 16ᵗʰ Div Sigls. and new Lodgeform on 3 animals. (Eye cream)	Animals Admitted
	20ᵗʰ		8/14S to ASC. Evacuated 8 animals (1 on foot) (M7 Indus.) to No 23 V.H. 1 RCO up hand L	2 (Cross 8)
	21ˢᵗ		Capt Parker & Pte Martin to new area. Capt Parker to select site for camp.	3
	22		Limber to Lebrage dump with unserviceable clothing retiring.	1
	23ʳᵈ		Evacuated 6 animals to No 23 VH (men on foot) Party to return same day J17 b 8.3. Ration wagon collected Section moved from D19.d.6.6. to Winnezeele J17 b 8.3. Surplus forage &c and followed on to new camp.	1 Cross 6)
	24ᵗʰ		Capt Parker inspected animals of Albert W15, 8ᵗʰ Dublin 112 L Fd Ambulance 4 14 to RE. Evacuation Party with Pack brought on load of stores from old camp. Lt Geoffroy & Pte Reece to take charge of Rest Horse Lieut at J.6.a.1.4., 2 Arthurstown drying hurd saddle horses. Capt Parker with Lt DVS to Sear area to select site for camp.	3
	25ᵗʰ		Hurt Spur to 1ˢᵗ/1ˢᵗ Capt A.V.D. with one animal. Pte Downie returned from leave.	2 Cross 1)

WAR DIARY
or
INTELLIGENCE SUMMARY

Army Form C. 2118.

47th Mobile Veterinary Section 16th Division

July 1917

Place	Date	Hour	Summary of Events and Information	Remarks and references to Appendices
WATOU K.5.a.9.7 July 26/7/17			Section moved from WINNEZEELE J.17.B.8.3. to WATOU K.5.a.9.7.	Amended
	27th		Capt Smits to D.A.D.V.S. conference with returns. Capt Smits to H.Q. 48th Infty Bde. re dressing Sgt. in place of Pte. Carrington. Pte. Shepherd to H.Q. 48th Infty Bde. 4/112 Field Ambulance.	1
	28th		Capt Smits to inspect animals of H.Q. 48th Infty Bde. Remounts for coal. Capt Smits to rear area to select site for camp, also inspected animals of 9th Dublins & 143rd Bn. C.R.E.	1
	29th		Capt Smits to rear area to select site for camp	2
	30th		Section moved from K.5.a.9.7. WATOU to G.14.b.3.5. Poperinghe. 7.30 pm to 11.30 pm	1
	31st	9.30am	Remise to Horse Shelt J.6.a.1.4. for Lt Sopfry to Rieuce (reopening section) rest at 3 pm. 16th D.A.C. 2 from 1st S.C. R.E. 51 Animals collected on that 3 pm	7

Lieut Col Ralph (Contracted) for Mange dressing 12 Gallons Grease were used during the month.

Total Animals Admitted	37
do Evacuated	19
do Cases Returned	13
do Died Destroyed	2

[signature] Winter Capt
O.C. 47th M.V.S.

WAR DIARY.

FOR MONTH OF AUGUST, 1917.

VOLUME 21

UNIT 47th Mobile Vety Section
A.V.C.

Army Form C. 2118.

WAR DIARY H.Q. N. Mobile Veterinary Section
or
INTELLIGENCE SUMMARY. 16th Div.
(Erase heading not required.)

August 1917

Place	Date	Hour	Summary of Events and Information	Remarks and references to Appendices
POPERINGHE				
Gbr b.3.5.	Aug 1st/917		Pte. Hoar to 113th S.A.R.B. for mule, sent mover Army Right River Ordnance Depot. Capt Sanders visited horse lines of 49th S.A. Bde. Evacuated 1 animal per post to III Corps M.V.S.	1
	Aug 2nd		Evacuated 9 animals (2 on foot) to II CMVD. Limber to ordnance for tent. Wagon to R.B. Dump for material. Section moved from Poperinghe to H.17.C.3.4. near Krinshoet. Animal C13237. Destroyed. Animal buried.	1
		30	Wagon returned to Poperinghe for remainder of stores. Stores collected.	2.5
			Mule (wounded) of 11th Sh.Sher.(?) 30th Div	
	4th		Cpl Blackburn took over duties of A.V.C. Pte. to H.Q. Inf Bde. in place of Pte. Ulpheston granted leave	8
	5th		Pte. Ulpheston granted leave Aug 7th to 17th. 1 Pte. to Station to bring horse feed	9
	6th		99y 1 Pte to 15th to Horse lines to assist in disinfection. returned 3pm. 1 animal to II Corps M.V.D. On return Pte collected another case. Evacuated 1 animal to II Corps M.V.D. On return Pte collected another case.	4
			Dvr Hogarth granted leave Aug 9th to 17th. 1 Pte. to Stn. to bring back horse ev(?)acted	11

T2134. Wt. W708—776. 500000. 4/15. Sir J.C. & S.

Army Form C. 2118.

WAR DIARY
or
INTELLIGENCE SUMMARY.
(Erase heading not required.)

Place	Date	Hour	Summary of Events and Information	Remarks and references to Appendices
#1.V.C.S.4 hrs KRUISSTRAAT	Aug 7th 1917		Lectrin moves from advanced post to Poperinghe B.14.B.6.4. I Off. and Remitter	Animals Remitter
			3 hours left S.o., for charges of Advanced Collecting Station, all walking cases, brought away. Owing to Artillery to await, and 1 animal brought in float	15
Poperinghe B.14.B.6.4.	Aug 8th		Off. hacker, Major to advanced collecting Station, for 1 horse. 16 horses walking cases brought in. Late float returned to A.C. Station for 1 horse. Capt Renton to A.C. Stn to inspect animals admitted. Animal C13.5/3. of 16th Div Sy Co. collected from float	20
	9th		Float to Adv.Stn. for 1 horse, later collected 3 animals from D.A.C. then to Aberdeen with rations. brought in 2 animals. Party for 16 walking cases from Rir.Stn. Capt Renton to D.A.D.V.S. +D.H.Q. to arrange for assistance in view, too many animals in for depleted section Personnel	22
	10th		Evacuated 3 animals by float to II.C.A.V.D. and 48 by road to D.Omer. float collected 1 animal from Junction Stn from C/177 R.F.A. Capt Renton to II.C.A.V.D. to arrange for large evacuation of horses	63 Evacuated 51

WAR DIARY
or
INTELLIGENCE SUMMARY

Army Form C. 2118.

HQ Mobile Veterinary Section

No. ..O/113.......... Date ..21/9/17..

Place	Date	Hour	Summary of Events and Information	Remarks and references to Appendices
Opsomers E.14.6.4.4	Aug 11th/1917		Went to 2nd Lee D.A.C. for Zemaphs, later to B180 collected sick, brought Admitted in Zemaphs from Amb Stations. Lander to Reinforce with rations Forage	Animals 28
	12th		Capt Renton to Reinforce to inspect Admittances and to 113th Field Ambulance. 1 Bn 44th Men of Artillery Evgh attached Emburton lines. Evacuated 1 Animal by train to II C.A.V.D. 3 Section Riders returned from II C.A.V.D. Lander to Reinforce with Rations & Pts of injured Section brought in to Amb. C.B.A.P. 272. 265. 363. 403. Destinges only one carcase suitable for skinning	11
	13th		Evacuated 100 animals (Humphreys) to II Corps M.V.D. A.D.V.S. and D.A.D.V.S. Inspected. Some before evacuation Lander to Ordnance for stores Capt Renton to II C.A.V.D. with evacuation papers	10
	14th		Evacuated 48 Animal by train to El Omer. 1 Batn Horses (Compl. Arti.) returned to Unit Lemnos destinges skinned & Buried. Wagon to PEESL HOEK for Cartridges Cylinders one hose taken in to II CM.V.D.	45
				149 EVACTD

WAR DIARY
or
INTELLIGENCE SUMMARY.

Army Form C. 2118.

Place	Date	Hour	Summary of Events and Information	Remarks and references to Appendices
Poperinghe 6.4 R.6.H	Aug 15/17	11	Wagon to Reselhoek for 75 Cartridge Cylinders, taken on to II Corps A.D.S.	Animals Admitted
			Horse brought in 3 Animals from advanced collecting station.	63
	16th	8.30a	Horse collected 2 animals from arm.Sn. later brought in one from 18th DAC.	44
			2 Ptes sent for duty at adv.Sn. and 6 animals brought in	
	17th		1 Pte to A.D.M.S. for H.Q. and Classification (Category "A" or)	
			Evacuated 2.5 animals to II Cps 2 D. 5 Taken in from (Animal C13449	13
			Limbs to office of A.D.V.S. XIX Corps for Very Anxous G.S. Destroyed Skinned & Buried)	
	18th		2 Animals C.B.605 392" Destroyed Skinned Buried. Evacuated 114 Animals to II Cps 2 D	9
			3 taken in Host. Horse collected animal from Q.177 Bde R.F.A. and later	
			brought in two Cases from arm Sn. Wagon to A.S.C. for Stores Forage	
			1 Pte returned from leave.	

Evac 139

Army Form C. 2118.

WAR DIARY
or
INTELLIGENCE SUMMARY.
(Erase heading not required.)

47th MOBILE SECTION. A.V.C. No. 9/113 Date 4/9/17

Place	Date	Hour	Summary of Events and Information	Remarks and references to Appendices
Poperinghe.	Aug 19/1917		Went to II Corps M.V.D. with 9 Horses. Limber to Car Stn to bring in Sgt W/c. and Stores. Horse brought in 2 animals from Car Stn, 1 left and arrangements made with returning M.V.S. to collect. Animals handed over. Section moved from Poperinghe E14.b.6.4. to Watou K.1.a.9.7. Horse to follow on later. Wagon returned to Poperinghe for stores. Capt Sanders acting for D.A.V.S. on leave.	Animals Admitted — 1
	20th		Pres. A.V.S. returned from leave. Limber to Ordnance for Stores and take to O.C. XIX Corps returning to tents. Wagon to Salvage dump with surplus stores. Capt Sanders to Wormhoudt to inspect animals of 10th Battn. Ration wagon with three horses from Deal Train, attached Section for move.	2
	21st		Evacuated 5 animals to II Ch.V.D. and left two horses to travel at Farm Section left Watou K.1.a.9.7. 11.30pm for Caestre Station arrived 3am 22nd	4
	22nd		Entrained and left Caestre 6.30am, arrived and detrained Bapaume Station 2pm, travelled to camp Achiet les Petits, arrived 5.30pm	— Evac. St.

Army Form C. 2118.

WAR DIARY or INTELLIGENCE SUMMARY.

(Erase heading not required.)

47th MOBILE SECTION, A.V.C.
No. 9/113
Date 2/9/17

Place	Date	Hour	Summary of Events and Information	Remarks and references to Appendices
Achiet le Petit	Aug 23/17		Capt Senton to H.Q. duties of D.A.D.V.S.	Animals Admitted
	24/25		General cleaning up Horses Saddlery Vehicles putting Camp in order.	
	26th		2 Sergeants granted leave Aug 26th to Sep 9th	1
	27th		Return moved from Achiet le Petit to Bihucourt Ricinode 1-30pm to 7-30pm	1
			Took over 9 sick animals from 33rd M.V.S. Offset wheel broken on leaving last camp	9
	28th		wagon returned for float load of stores.	4
	29th		1 Pte Granted leave Aug 31st to Sept 10th	6
	30th		1 Cpl rejoined Section from III Corps Sn V.R.	3
	31st		1 Cpl with wagon to Miraumont to pick up above. 3 Pte with Pte awaiting Conveyance 10am to 11.20 pm	3
			kicks to Ordnance for stores.	

Animals Admitted during month   423
Cured & Returned   1 2
Died or Destroyed   1 6
Evacuated   355

D Senton
Capt
O.C. 47 Mob V.S.

2/9/17.

WAR DIARY.

FOR MONTH OF SEPTEMBER, 1917.

VOLUME 22

UNIT:- 4yth Mobile Veterinary Secn
AVC

Army Form C. 2118.

WAR DIARY
or
INTELLIGENCE SUMMARY.
(Erase heading not required.)

September 47th Mobile Veterinary Section 16th Division

Instructions regarding War Diaries and Intelligence Summaries are contained in F. S. Regs., Part II. and the Staff Manual respectively. Title pages will be prepared in manuscript.

O/219 3/10/17

Place	Date	Hour	Summary of Events and Information	Remarks and references to Appendices
BOIRY. ST RICTRUDE. S14. Sheet 51 B.	1/9/17		Capt Fenton resumed section duty as acting D.A.D.V.S. completed	Animals admitted
		1 pm.	Party of 1 NCO 4 Men to ACHIET LES PETIT to load broken feet on to Lillefin, rept 6 pm	8
			1 NCO to S.O. Dir. A.V.S. for instruction in use of vapour baths for mange treatment	
			1 Pte to Hellen 47th Inf Bde as relief to A.V.C. Pte proceeding on leave	
	2nd			2
	3rd		2 Pte to Horse Dip (Range) MONDICOURT for duty	
	4th		Evacuation by train to Forceville Essex 18 Animals. 1 NCO 4 Men i/c.	1
			1 NCO to assist in disinfection of horse standings of 1 & 6 H.T. Cos R.E. at ST JULIAN	8
			3 Pte (Mounted) to ACHIET LES GRAND Rly Park for loading up motor lorries with material for section stabling and huts	
	5th		Capt Fenton inspected CBSD/19 and extracted pieces of shrapnel	
			Evacuation party of 3rd returned 3 H.S. Am...	
			Capt Fenton inspected animals of H/S Supply Col at ERVILLERS & HAMELINCOURT. Lorries to GUINCHES for Motorwheels for repair.	8
	6th		Captain Fenton to BEETENCOURT to inspect animals of 20th Reserve Park	15
				EVAC. 18

Army Form C. 2118.

47th MOBILE SECTION, A.V.C.
No.
Date Sept/1917

WAR DIARY
or
INTELLIGENCE SUMMARY.

(Erase heading not required.)

Instructions regarding War Diaries and Intelligence Summaries are contained in F.S. Regs., Part II. and the Staff Manual respectively. Title pages will be prepared in manuscript.

Place	Date	Hour	Summary of Events and Information	Remarks and references to Appendices
BOIRY ST. RICTRUDE.	7/9/17.		1 Offr to VI Corps H.Q. BIHUCOURT. to collect animal (Range Case)	Animals Admitted 1
	8th		Limbers to Ordnance for stores and to S.O.M.V.S. for lime. 2 Offrs returned from leave. Wgn to Canadian Saw-Mill for dust.	2
	9th		Wgn to Canadian Saw-Mill for dust. 1 Offr granted leave. (10 days) Limber to Ordnance for stores	8
	10th		Evacuated by train 3 animals 1 RCO taken Pte. Limber to RE Park BOYELLES for material. Crew of Dural Shutting Co attached, for erection of Section Shelby and huts.	5
	11th		1 Pte returned from leave.	3
	12th		Limber to RE Park Boyelles for nails etc	5
	13th		Evacuation party of 10th returned 3am.	4
	14th		1 Offr to Divl Signal Co BEHAGNIES to collect STRAY animal. Limber to Ordnance for stores. Capt Fenton inspected animals of 448th Siege Bty Rda and 143 C.C.S	8

EVAC. 38

Army Form C. 2118.

WAR DIARY
or
INTELLIGENCE SUMMARY.
(Erase heading not required.)

47th MOBILE SECTION A.V.C.
Sept / 1917.

Place	Date	Hour	Summary of Events and Information	Remarks and references to Appendices
BOIRY ST RICTRUDE	15/9/17			Animals Admitted
			Capt Senton to horse dep HONDICOURT to supervise clipping of horses of one Coy of Div Train.	2
			Capt Senton inspected all animals of Divl Train.	
			Wagon to Dump for coal.	
	16th		NCO & 3 men (mounted) to ACHIET LES GRAND to load lorries with stabling material	7
	17th			
	18th		Evacuated 36 animals by train to FORQUEVES EPUX 1 NCO 4 men etc.	5
	19th		Evacuation party of 17th returned 7.15 pm. 1 Cpl granted 10 days leave	1
	20th		Capt Senton inspected animals of 2nd R.D.F. at ERVILLERS and held destruction on animal (alice)	2
			Capt Senton to DADVS weekly conference at MOYENVILLE	2
	21st		1 Otr returned from leave	
			Wagon to BOYELLES for building material	7
	22nd		Evacuated 16 animals 1 NCO 4 men etc. Wagon for building material	8

EVAC 54

Army Form C. 2118.

WAR DIARY
or
INTELLIGENCE SUMMARY.
(Erase heading not required.)

47th MOBILE SECTION. A.V.C.
Date: Sept / 1917.

Place	Date	Hour	Summary of Events and Information	Remarks and references to Appendices
BOIRY ST RICTRUDE	23/9/17		Wagon to BRETENCOURT for Land.	Animals Admitted 2
	24th		Evacuating Party of 2nd Division 3.30 a.m. Evacuated 5 animals by train to FORGES LES EAUX 1 A.C.D. S/c	5
	25th		Wagon to BRETENCOURT for Land. Evacuated 8 animals 1 A.C.D. S/c.	5
	26th		Wagon to BRETENCOURT for Land.	13
	27th		Capt Lenton to D.A.D.V.S.'s weekly conference. Wagon to BRETENCOURT for Land.	2
	28th		1 O.R. granted 10 days leave. Capt Lenton and 1 A.C.D. to Headquarters, animal to be operated on.	18
	29th		Evacuated 32 animals by train to Forges Les Eaux. 1 A.C.D. + 3 Men S/c E.Wagon to D.A.D.V.S. office.	4 EVAC 48

WAR DIARY or INTELLIGENCE SUMMARY.

Army Form C. 2118.

47th MOBILE SECTION A.V.C.
Sept/1917.

Place	Date	Hour	Summary of Events and Information	Remarks and references to Appendices
BOIRY St RICTRUDE	30/9/17		1 Cpl returned from leave	Animals admitted 2.
			40 Gallons of Hy Cal. Sulph. contracted. made and issued during the month.	
			Animals Admitted 160	
			do Evacuated 158	
			do Cured & Issued 23	
			do Died or Destroyed nil.	
			do. Remaining 20	

(sig) Boylan
Capt. A.V.C.
O.C. 47th M.V.S.

WAR DIARY

FOR MONTH OF OCTOBER, 1917.

UNIT 4th Mob. Vet. Sec. A.V.C.

VOLUME NUMBER 23

WAR DIARY or INTELLIGENCE SUMMARY.

Army Form C. 2118.

49th Mobile Veterinary Section / 16th Div.

Place	Date	Hour	Summary of Events and Information	Remarks and references to Appendices
BORY ST RICTRUDE Sheet 51 B S.I.H. C.6.K.	1/4/17	9.45 am	1 Pte to Corps Horse Dep as relief for Pte proceeding on leave. At Stables. One dispatch (ASC) Ricker by horse, was taken in. Motor Ambulance to 112th Field Ambulance. Mules to No 20 C.C.S.	1
	2/4/17		Evacuation Party of 1/29 returned.	1
	3rd		Evacuated 16 animals to No 7 Vety Hospital FORGES LES EAUX (by train). Evacuation Party. 1 RCD orphan o/c.	1
	4th		Horse collected animal CB No 236 from Erinsford. 1 Pte granted 10 days leave. 1/3 returned.	4
	5th		Wagon to BERVILLE for load of sand, late to Oranena for stores. 1 Pte granted 10 days leave.	3
	6th		Wagon to BERVILLE for load of sand. Evacuated 13 animals. 1 NCO 4 men o/c.	1

Evac 27.

WAR DIARY
INTELLIGENCE SUMMARY
(Erase heading not required.)

Army Form C. 2118.

Place	Date	Hour	Summary of Events and Information	Remarks and references to Appendices
	7/9/17		Went to MOYENVILLE for annual C13 Stue. Later to BONLEUX & Mt Mastutst	Annuals
			for C13 H6. ASC transport driver reported. Replace Casualty	3
	8th		Lorries to ERVILLERS for coal woods	3
			Evacuation Staff Officer	
	9th		Capt Newton inspected animals of 448 Infantry Base	2
	10th		Wagon to BLAIRVILLE for 2 loads of sand	4
	11th		Lorries to Ochanese for stores.	8
	12th		Lorries to Ochanese for stores. 1 Pte returned from leave	1
	13th		Wagon for time for fire buckets. Lorries to R.E. Park BOYELLES for Pickets. Evacuated 16 animals (3 to neither in front) 1 NCO 2 men s/c	6
			1 Driver returned from leave.	
				EVAC 14

Army Form C. 2118.

WAR DIARY
or
INTELLIGENCE SUMMARY.
(Erase heading not required.)

Place	Date	Hour	Summary of Events and Information	Remarks and references to Appendices
	14/10/19		Annual C106 & 061 died. Post mortem by Capt Fenton. Carcase skinned & buried. Arm? 2	Answer 2, 3
			Wagon for Coal Corpl.	
	15th		Evacuation party of 13th returned. Evacuated 9 animals, 1 RCD & then K	1
	16th		Evacuation party of 15th returned	1
	17th		Hat collected animal C156 & 294 from Engineers. Sunk to BRETENCOURT. Wagon & Drivers for Hay. 1 Oth returned from leave	3
	18th		Staff Sgt granted 10 days leave. 1 Oth returned from leave	5
	19th		Sunk to BOYELLES for oral report. Lorry to Ordnance for stores to RE Park BOYELLES for 2 loads of building material	6
	20th		Evacuated 9 animals, 6 RCD & 1 PC O/c	6

WAR DIARY
or
INTELLIGENCE SUMMARY.
(Erase heading not required.)

Army Form C. 2118.

Instructions regarding War Diaries and Intelligence Summaries are contained in F. S. Regs., Part II and the Staff Manual respectively. Title pages will be prepared in manuscript.

Place	Date	Hour	Summary of Events and Information	Remarks and references to Appendices
	21/10/17		Wagon to ERVILLERS for Hay	Private Admitted 4
	22nd		Evacuated 14 Animals. 1 hCO ÷ 2 Ptes Ye. Limber to Ordnance for Stores. 6 Pte granted 10 days leave	3
	23rd		Evacuation Party of 20 Pte returned. Horses to HAMELIN COURT for Annual Chgo.	5
	24th		Wagon with trailing limber to Favreuil. Limber to ERVILLERS for Hay. Pte collected Animal CBh° 909 from ERVILLERS. Evacuation Party of 25 returned.	6
	25th		Wagon to Ordnance for Stores. Cart to BARASTRE for sand. 10 Pte granted 10 days leave. 1 Pte returned from Class	3
	26th		Pte collected Animal CBh° 913 from ERVILLERS. 1 Cpl to DaDVVS Office for temp'y duty as clerk. Limber to BOYELLES for cart wood	7, 2
	27th		Evacuated 16 Animals. 1hCO ÷ 2 Ptes Ye	3

W.H.

Army Form C. 2118.

WAR DIARY
or
INTELLIGENCE SUMMARY.
(Erase heading not required.)

Instructions regarding War Diaries and Intelligence Summaries are contained in F. S. Regs., Part II. and the Staff Manual respectively. Title pages will be prepared in manuscript.

Place	Date	Hour	Summary of Events and Information	Remarks and references to Appendices
	28/10/17		Limbers to KENNELS for hay	Summary Attached 1
	29th		Wagon to BEAUVAL for 2 loads of sand	2
	30th		Limbers to Ordnance for stores. Wagon to R.E. Park BOYELLES for material. Staff/S1 returned from leave	3
	31st		Evacuated 32 animals. 1 N.C.O. + 3 Ptes. H. Wagon to KENNELS for hay Limbers to R.E. Park for hutting material. Stores collected from HAMELINCOURT.	35
			83/2 Gallons (Concentrated) of L.I.Q. Cal. Sol. P.H. Auto issued during the month.	
			Arundlo admitted 149	
			" Cases Dieoff 15	
			" Died Destroyed 1	
			" Evacuated 125	
			" Remaining 52	

D. Braxton
W. Oph
Oct 29th /17.

WAR DIARY

FOR MONTH OF NOVEMBER, 1917.

VOLUME : - 24

UNIT :- 4½ Mobile Veterinary Sec. A.V.C.

WAR DIARY or INTELLIGENCE SUMMARY

Army Form C. 2118.

November 1917

17 Mobile Veterinary Section
16th Division

Place	Date	Hour	Summary of Events and Information	Remarks and references to Appendices
STN. C.6.4. BOISLEUX ST. MARC	1/11/17		Capt Linton to inspect site for Veterinary Aid Post at 727.C.9.4. (Sh:57B) near ST LEGER.	Animals Admitted
			Wagon to BOIRY VILLE for one load sand	2
	2nd		1 Cpl + 4 Pts to Veterinary Aid Post. Lorries with stores etc.	37
			Wagon for coal wood	
	3rd		Animal CB No 9444 died during night. Post manned by Capt Linton. Later unease	1
			Skinned & buried. Wagon to V.A.P. with rations.	
			1 Pte returned from leave.	
	4th		Number to Ordnance for Stores. Wagon to KERVILLERS for Hay.	4
	5th		Evacuated 16 animals. 1 Opl + 10 men S/B. Number to V.A.P. with Rations + Water.	15
	6th		1 Sch. 16 painted ten days leave. Number to Ordnance for stores.	12
	7th		Wagon to Advanced Post with rations. Cpl Stephens reported sick from S.A.R. (Seg Set) Evacuation party of 3 returned	5
	8th		1 Pte returned from leave	
			Shot selected animal C.B.No 418 from ABLAINZEVILLE	5
	9th		Wagon to R.E. Post Bayeller for stores. Limbers to Volupliedbat with rations. Wagon for coal wood.	1
			Evacuated 37 animals (1 infoal) RCD vys ram 3/c	Total 90 Evac. 93

WAR DIARY
INTELLIGENCE SUMMARY

Army Form C. 2118.

Place	Date	Hour	Summary of Events and Information	Remarks and references to Appendices
Boisle St Richard	10/11/17		Wagon to Blainville for 2 loads of Sand. Limber to R.E. Park for material	— 7
			Flat collected animal C13.20.58 from HAMELINCOURT	3
	11th		Limber to R.E. Park for petrol. Wagon to V.A.P with rations and later for Vererinary	— 31
	12th		NCO & Pte to collect animal Cuff with Son Major GONIECOURT. Flat collected animal C13.62	— 8
			Limber to Ordnance for Stores	
	13th		Capt Fenton Inspected all animals of Sup. Coy Coe	— 8
	14th		Wagon to Blainville for 2 loads Sand. Limber to V.A.P with sick horse	
			Wagon to Ecurie for hay. Evacuated 24 animals (Horses)	3
			NCO & Men Ptes. Flat to ordnance for Vererinary Aid Post. Capt Fenton to Vererinary Aid Post	
	15th		Limber to Tr. Hen's workshop for Muleo horse for M.T. 2 Ptes (mounted) with spare horses to horse dep MONDICOURT, to bring sick horses on detached duty	12
			NCO & Men of Divisional Shifting Co returned to units 1 Ptes of Ammunition Sup animal died same day	
			Flat collected C13.R°90 from	
	16th		Evacuated 11 animals 1 R°84 of man the Post Mortem by Capt Fenton on animal C13.90. Labs carcase skinned burned Flat Collected C13.111 from AVESNES	19
	19th		Flat collected C13.111 from AVESNES. Limber to Ordnance for Stores	Total - 63 Evac - 35

WAR DIARY or INTELLIGENCE SUMMARY.

Army Form C. 2118.

Place	Date	Hour	Summary of Events and Information	Remarks and references to Appendices
BOIRY Ste RICTRUDE	18/11/17		Wagon to V.A.P. with rations. Mules to ERVILLERS for stores.	1 animal admitted
	19th		Evacuated 16 animals. 1 NCO & 1 man sick.	
			Mules to V.A.P. with rations & seeds.	1
	20th		Capt. Linton to V.A.P.	
	21st		Evacuated 16 animals. 1 NCO & 1 man sick. Wagon to V.A.P. with rations.	1
			Evacuation Party of 19th returned.	
	22nd		Wagon to Berles-au-Bois for 1 load of hay.	1
	23rd		Limber to V.A.P. with rations. Later, to Ordnance, Croisilles.	
			Wagon & cob stored. Evacuation Party of 21st returned.	5
			Wagon to V.A.P. for rations etc. 1 Pte & 1 recruit returned from leave.	
			1 Pte rejoined section (post closed).	
	24th		Float to Bland Dump with unservicable surplus clothing etc.	3
			Wagon for 1 load of hay. 1 OR admitted to 7th field ambulance.	
	25th		Wagon to Blainville for 2 loads of sand.	1
	26th		Evacuated 11 animals. 1 NCO & 1 man sick. That col. returns animal OB.158.	2
			Mules to Railhead for hay. Pupts. Rt. from N.2 Vety Hospital Rouen.	

Total — 20.
Evac — 23

Army Form C. 2118.

WAR DIARY
or
INTELLIGENCE SUMMARY.
(Erase heading not required.)

Instructions regarding War Diaries and Intelligence Summaries are contained in F. S. Regs., Part II. and the Staff Manual respectively. Title pages will be prepared in manuscript.

Place	Date	Hour	Summary of Events and Information	Remarks and references to Appendices
Army H.Q. Rokinda	27/11/19		Limbers to Wynberg 17th Bde RFA. Handed over T with Lieut Right Kit	Appendix attached
			Wagon for 1 load of hay	1
	28th		Wagon to Blenville for 2 loads hay	3
	29th		Contradicted T.Pn 2 from lines of 10th R. Dublin 820	
			Limber to 8 Remounts for Coal	4
	30th		Inspection of Western Cavalry reinforcements by GOCUT	
			Wages for week issued.	4
			Only 12 Gallons of M.T Oil Self (Concentrated) made and issued during the month:- Shortage of lime.)
			Advances for Section personnel animals drawn from Railhead as links by a vehicle
			during this journey daily.
			Animals Remaining last month — 28.
			" Admitted since — 163
			" Evacuated — 171
			" Cured Horses — 19
			" Died or Destroyed — 7
			" Remaining — 19

Burton Capt
O.C. 17th V.H

WAR DIARY,

FOR MONTH OF DECEMBER, 1917.

VOLUME :- 25

UNIT :- 4/th Mobile Veterinary Section
A.V.C.

Vol 24

Army Form C. 2118.

WAR DIARY
or
INTELLIGENCE SUMMARY.
(Erase heading not required.)

No. **16th DIVISION**

Instructions regarding War Diaries and Intelligence Summaries are contained in F. S. Regs., Part II. and the Staff Manual respectively. Title pages will be prepared in manuscript.

Place	Date	Hour	Summary of Events and Information	Remarks and references to Appendices
BOI RY. ST.	2/12/14		1 Sergeant and 2 Corporals to No 9 Vet Corps Salvage to give evidence on wounded man.	
R. ST. RUDE	3/12/14		Evacuated 116 Animals to No 4 Veterinary Hospital	
	4/12/14	10:30AM	Section moved from Boiry-St-Ridines to Rouyal-court, arrived 8-30 P.M. everything correct.	
Rouyal-court	5/12/14	9AM	Section moved from Rouyal-court to Villers-Aucon.	
			Arrived Villers-Aucon 2.30 P.M. everything correct	
Villers-Aucon	7/12/14	9AM	Section moved into VII Corps D.b.S. standings.	
			Evacuated 138 animals to No 4 Veterinary Hospital	
	8/12/14	1.P.M.	Mounted Orderly to report at VII Corps H.D.S. Daily	
			4" M.V.S. with personnel attached building ½ repairing stables	
	9/12/14		at V.b.b.S. Capt W Cawthorne appointed O.C. vice Capt W Leuton AVC	
		5 P.M	Orderly to D.A.D.V.S. with Daily state.	
	11/12/14		Evacuated 180 animals to No 4 Veterinary Hospital	
	13/12/14	1:30AM	Conducting party returned from No 4 Veterinary Hospital	
	14/12/14		2 Sergeants + 1 Pte inoculated with T.A.B. at No 2 Field Ambulance	
			Evacuated 103 animals to No 4 Veterinary Hospital	

W. Cawthorne Capt AVC

Army Form C. 2118.

WAR DIARY
or
INTELLIGENCE SUMMARY.
(Erase heading not required.)

Instructions regarding War Diaries and Intelligence Summaries are contained in F. S. Regs., Part II. and the Staff Manual respectively. Title pages will be prepared in manuscript.

Place	Date	Hour	Summary of Events and Information	Remarks and references to Appendices
Villers-Bocage	15/12/14		2 Animals were destroyed skinned and buried	
	17/12/14		About for animal from 143 Army M.S.C. Chge 18D	
	18/12/14		Evacuated 94 Animals to No 4 Veterinary Hospital	
	20/12/14		About to Sand-court for animal	
	21/12/14		Evacuated 56 animals to No 4 Veterinary Hospital	
			Returned to Base men to No 5 Veterinary Hospital	
"	22/12/14		4th M.V.S. and attached personnel repairing stables & lines	
"	23/12/14	1.30 PM	Conducting party returned from No 4 Veterinary Hospital	
"	24			
"	25		4th M.V.S. and attached, repairing stables, and making fresh lines to sick animals	
"	26			
"	27			
"	28		Evacuated 109 animals to No 4 Veterinary Hospital	
"	29	2 PM	W.O. 1 men parade for duties	
"	30		About for animal from D 189 A.F.A. Bde CB 304 West Riding div	

W. Carr Kept

Army Form C. 2118.

WAR DIARY
or
INTELLIGENCE SUMMARY.
(Erase heading not required.)

Instructions regarding War Diaries and Intelligence Summaries are contained in F. S. Regs., Part II. and the Staff Manual respectively. Title pages will be prepared in manuscript.

Place	Date	Hour	Summary of Events and Information	Remarks and references to Appendices
Ddlinstaween	31/10/18		About 15 D 382 P.F.A. bn. for renewal. CB 363.	
"	1/11/18 to 30/11/18		Working parties of R.E. burying in water supplys, to watering animals at L.L.L.	

W Cawthorn Capt.
R.A.V.C. My V.S.
IIth Div.

WAR DIARY,

FOR MONTH OF JANUARY, 1918.

VOLUME :- 26

UNIT :- 47th Mobile Vety. Sec. A.V.C.

Army Form C. 2118.

WAR DIARY
or
INTELLIGENCE SUMMARY.

(Erase heading not required.)

Instructions regarding War Diaries and Intelligence Summaries are contained in F. S. Regs., Part II. and the Staff Manual respectively. Title pages will be prepared in manuscript.

Place	Date	Hour	Summary of Events and Information	Remarks and references to Appendices
VILLERS – FANCON	1/1/18	9 A.M.	Evacuated 45 animals to N° 4 Veterinary Hospital.	
	2/1/18	11-30 A.M.	S/Sgt Winteley and 9 men to Boronne to bring remounts from station to 4ᵗʰ Mobile Veterinary Section	
do	3/1/18			
do	4/1/18		Evacuated 48 animals to N° 4 Veterinary Hospital.	
do	8/1/18	9 A.M.	Evacuated 125 animals to N° 4 Veterinary Hospital	
do			1 Staff Sergeant + man Inoculated with $\frac{TAB}{2}$ at 113 Field Ambulance.	
do	9/1/18	11 A.M.	About to D 180 Bde R.F.A. for animal.	
do	11/1/18	9 A.M.	Evacuated 56 animals to N° 4 Veterinary Hospital	
do	13/1/18	10 A.M.	About to 4 Bay. ASC 21ˢᵗ Div. for animal.	
do	15/1/18	9 A.M.	Evacuated 50 animals to N° 4 Veterinary Hospital.	
do			About for animal to 16ᵗʰ D.A.C.	
do	18/1/18	9 A.M.	Evacuated 30 animals to N° 4 Veterinary Hospital	
do	22/1/18	9 A.M.	Evacuated 59 animals to N° 4 Veterinary Hospital	
do	24/1/18	10 A.M.	About for animal from C 144 Bde R.F.A.	
do	25/1/18		About for animal from 94 Field Company R.E. + W. Section 21 D.A.C.	

Army Form C. 2118.

WAR DIARY
or
INTELLIGENCE SUMMARY.

(Erase heading not required.)

Instructions regarding War Diaries and Intelligence
Summaries are contained in F. S. Regs., Part II.
and the Staff Manual respectively. Title pages
will be prepared in manuscript.

Place	Date	Hour	Summary of Events and Information	Remarks and references to Appendices
VILLERS - FANCON	20/1/18	8 AM	Report Directly to VII Corps H.Q. A.D.V.S to act as blank.	
do	29/1/18	8 AM	Orderly to A.D.V.S VII Corps Evacuated 39 animals to Mobⁿ Veterinary Hospital	
do			2 B/os to build stabling at "A.D.V.S" TINCOURT	
do	31/1/18	2 PM	Moved to HIZECOURT W/2 Coy. A.S.C. 21st Div. for arrival	

W. Caruthers
Capt
O.C 4 4th Mobile
Veterinary Section

Vol 26

WAR DIARY.

FOR MONTH OF FEBRUARY, 1918.

VOLUME:- 27

UNIT:- 47th Mobile Veterinary Section. A.V.C.

16 Division

Army Form C. 2118.

WAR DIARY
or
INTELLIGENCE SUMMARY.

(Erase heading not required.)

February 1918.

Instructions regarding War Diaries and Intelligence Summaries are contained in F. S. Regs., Part II. and the Staff Manual respectively. Title pages will be prepared in manuscript.

Place	Date	Hour	Summary of Events and Information	Remarks and references to Appendices
VILLERS FAUCON Feb 1/1918	1st		1 OR granted 14 days leave. Host collected arrival of 282 Aug Bde RGA	Entries admitted 5
	2nd		Evacuated 28 animals to No 7 Veterinary Hospital	8
	3rd		3 Ohs K dh horses at Corps Dep. 1 mounted orderly to HQ VII Corps. Host collected arrival from 2/91 Bde RGA. 21st Div. 1 RCO to Stables	6
	4th		of HQ 24th Inf Bde to disinfect same.	15
	5th		Evacuated 30 animals to No 7 VH. 1 RCO granted 14 days leave.	6
	6th		Host collected arrival of 14th E ASC 16th Div	9
	7th			11
	8th		Evacuated 20 animals to No 7 VH	6
	9th		Mounted orderly to VII Corps HQ.	3
	10th			11
	11th			14
	12th		Evacuated 33 animals to 67 No 7 VH.	6
	13th			7
	14th		1 RCO + 2 hors to Tincourt (new camp) to refence buildings. Host collected 1/mmed	9

Army Form C. 2118.

WAR DIARY
or
INTELLIGENCE SUMMARY.

(Erase heading not required.)

February 1918

Place	Date	Hour	Summary of Events and Information	Remarks and references to Appendices
VILLERS FAUCON				Animals Admitted
	Feb 15th/1918		Evacuated 20 animals to No 7 V.H. Sectn. moved from VILLERS FAUCON	
To TINCOURT				
	16th			2
	17th			1
	18th		First Collected Animal of 18th & C 16th Div. at Villers Faucon	15
	19th		Evacuated 16 animals to No 7 V.H.	3
	20th		1 RCO When to horse dipg at Bieuvillers. 1 RCO granted 14 days leave	9
	21st		1 RCO returned from VII Corps HQ.	15
	22nd		Evacuated 27 animals to No 7 V.H.	3
	23rd		Mounted Orderly to VII Corps HQ	9
	24th			10
	25th		1 Re-inoculated (1st Dose) 10 days interval for 2nd	3
	26th		Evacuated 17 animals to No 7 V.H. Wagon to R.E. dump for building material	3
	27th		Wagon to R.E. dump for building material	27
	28th		3 Rtn Mounted made two journeys to MB 16 DAC for surplus remounts.	
			Limbers to Salvage Dump, DADOS Store for fuel. Stock collected Animal Rcd Stn	1

W Cawthorn
Capt
OC No 17 MVS

WAR DIARY or INTELLIGENCE SUMMARY

Army Form C. 2118.

Place	Date	Hour	Summary of Events and Information	Remarks and references to Appendices
TINCOURT J34.c.5.2. Sheet 62C.	April 2/1918		Evacuated 23 animals to 107 V.H. 3 Pts. Y/c. Re no reinforcement to complete Section establishment arrived from 2-3-VH. 31 mules shot as unfit for work	Admitted 6
	2nd		Stables for sick animals in course of construction. Orderly to VII Corps HQ. Wagon to Villers Faucon for forage & Rations for stabling. 2 Offrs returned from leave.	1
	3rd		1 Offr. to Villers Faucon for demonstration of Stable B.D. Limber for 1 load of fuel. Evacuation party of 1st returned.	1
	4th		Host collected animals of A/117 See R.S.A. from Marquaix. Capt Carter to Peronne to lecture on Periodic Ophthalmia to all Veterinary Officers of VII Corps.	12
	5th		Evacuated 9 animals by train to R of V. Vet Hospl. Wagon Lines with heats for horse standings	3
	6th		Wagon Limber carrying troots for horse standings. Wagon to Longe, Barleux, Artillery R.S. dump	12
	7th		Evacuated 38 animals to VII Corps Vety Evacuating Station. at La Quinonche, Peronne.	26
			by road. 1 Sgt with mounted party Y/c. Heat to Villers Faucon for stray oats (wounded) this animal was evacuated same evening. Limber to Sermille for meat ration. Evacuation party of 5th returned. 1 Offr & 113 Such inhalers for inoculation against dax.	
	8th		1 Offr to Vet. service at Mill VII Corps. 1 A.P. Dating bat. 1 Offr reached Tincourt numbered O.D. 613	4

WAR DIARY

INTELLIGENCE SUMMARY.

(Erase heading not required.)

Army Form C. 2118.

March 1918

Place	Date	Hour	Summary of Events and Information	Remarks and references to Appendices
TINCOURT	Feb 9th 1918		Mounted Orderly to A.D.V.S. Hd. VII Corps. 1 Cpl. returned from leave	Animals Admitted 1
	10th		Wagon to R.E. dump for building materials	4
	11th		Evacuations 26 animals to VII Corps V.E.S. including 3 Horse Casts	21
	12th		3 Pte. for detached duty at VII Corps V.E.S.	2
	13th		Wagon for Coal went	6
	14th		Inspection by C.O.C. 16th Division + Staff. Evacuated 25 animals to VII Corps V.E.S.	16
	15th		S.M.A. re-mounted to Section Personnel, 9pm 1 Cpl to R.W. Colls. Jul. R.S. VILLERS FAUCON. Returned	2
	16th		Mr. D. Oriordy to A.D.V.S. VII Corps. 1 Cpl. prom'd a 15 days leave. Lumber to Ordnance for stores	6
	17th		Inspection by D.D.V.S., A.D.V.S., +DADVS	1
	18th		Evacuated animals to VII Corps V.E.S. 21 at 2.30, 10 at 4 pm, 4 at 6pm	19
	19th		Host collected animal from VILLERS FAUCON + took on to VII V.E.S.	
			Wagon Lumber for material for section stabling	3
	20th		Limber to Ordnance for stores	9
	21st		Heavy hostile shelling of TINCOURT Station section premises adjacent. Evacuated 11 animals	33
			to VII Corps V.E.S. at 2.30pm, 4 at 4.30pm Men in float as food in dugout. Out section moved	
			into open country between BUIRE + TINCOURT Wood at 6pm Evacuation Party remained Party remained party	W.6
			till 2 am on 22nd	

WAR DIARY / INTELLIGENCE SUMMARY

Army Form C. 2118.

47th MOBILE SECTION, A.V.C.
31/3/18

March 1918

Place	Date	Hour	Summary of Events and Information	Remarks and references to Appendices
Army HQn	Mch 22/18.		Shat to TINCOURT for host of intelligence stores. 1000 un Rations moved to premises	
			of VII Corps V.E.S. at LA QUINCONCHE PERONNE and handed over	5
		1st wounded animals		
	23rd		Remained party took over all sick animals of VII Corps V.E.S. to eastern of BRIE Station	1
			Remainder of Section with transport left PERONNE — 10 a.m. for BIACHES. Party arrived	
			Sick animals with 2/L entrained at BRIE. remained Section 7am at BIACHES and animals	
			more than 1 hour on to BRAY. Section arrived 2.30 pm to CAPPY. 5 pm Divisional	
			animals admitted + evacuated to BRAY. 10 pm. Section left CAPPY and marched until	
		3 pm	camped in open at K20.P.2. 9. Sheet 62D.	
	24th	9 pm	Section moved to MERICOURT L'ABBE. Arrived entirely K.17.5/fem. Sheet 62d noth	1
			# DADVS at Divisional Hd Qrs	
	25th	11md	Section moved to LA NEUVILLE nn Corbie. Greater Circle animals, situation to ORBE	7
	26	3 pm	Section moved to WARFUSÉE ABANCOURT. left open at 11 am for ref reference.	1
			N33 d. 9. 2. Sheet 62D arrived 4 pm.	
	27th		Remitted 51 animals of 6th Div. # 3 of 5th Army Hdrs. from FA noh n. K. Saleux	35
			Station (RTO) Motor Tracks Supply only allowed to evacuate animals Tuesdays Fridays	406

WAR DIARY
INTELLIGENCE SUMMARY

Army Form C. 2118.

March 1918

47th MOBILE SECTION, A.V.C. 31/3/18

Place	Date	Hour	Summary of Events and Information	Remarks and references to Appendices
Shell 62.D N33.d.9.2.	28/3/18		Mounted Orderly to SOLEUX RTO to request trucks for evacuation	Appendices Permitted
	29th		Evacuated 45 animals to No 7 Veterinary Hospital 1 N.C.O. i/c from S/c.	15
	30th	3 am	1 Sgt. and Horses to SOLEUX rail station to form a camp for reception of sick animals from the section in advanced area, took along 32 animals to await facilities for evacuation to Base	7 33
	31st		32 animals mentioned above were evacuated by train, then 10 animals evac. on to SOLEUX. Capt Cawthorn superintended evacuations. Evacuation Party S/Sgt. returned.	6
			Information as requested by Officer i/c A.V.C. Remnr Worklist vide. Memo No 17/259/18 dated 3/4/18 from Officer i/c AVC Base Records.	
A. 47th			Mobile Veterinary Section, was formed on Tuesday Sep 28th 1915 and left the Depot at WOOLWICH to join the 16th (Irish) Division at DEEPCUT from ALDERSHOT on same date	
			Embarked at SOUTHAMPTON for FRANCE on Dec 16th 1915	

W. Cawthorn Captain
O.C. 47 M.V.S.

WAR DIARY / INTELLIGENCE SUMMARY

APRIL 1918

Army Form C. 2118.

Vol 28

Place	Date	Hour	Summary of Events and Information	Remarks and references to Appendices
	April 1/1918	11 am	M.V. Section moved from Sheet 62 D. N 33 d 9.2 to LONGANEU arrived 1 pm.	Animals Admitted
			Detachment at rear post SAIEUX evacuated 10 animals by train, personnel & other than train party rejoined Section.	3
	2ⁿᵈ		2 O/Ms rejoined Section from VII Corps Vet. Yes, one O/Ms detached.	8
	3ʳᵈ		1 O/M by road to ABBEVILLE, with Horse Float, Horse/mule for sick or replacement. LONGANEU 6 am by road to SAIEUX arrived 9am – 5
			Section moved from Osso Road. Camp to an open. Evacuated 14 ams sick by road to PICQUIGNY.	
	4ᵗʰ		Section moved left SAIEUX 8.00 am arrived AMIENS 5.30 pm hurricane lamps evacuated 3 animals to PICQUIGNY –	
			O/M letter received from A.D.V.S. VII Corps re A.D.V.S. V/3/4/1 date 29/3/18	
			To B.R.D.V.S. 16ᵗʰ Division	
			I should be glad if you will convey to Officers & others, P.O. Workers of the 47ᵗʰ M.V.S. my appreciation of the work performed by them during the time they were on the 1ⁿ Corps. The conduct of all ranks and when dealing care shown to sick and wounded animals under trying conditions at TINCOURT	
			on March 21ˢᵗ was great praiseworthy.	
			(Signed) G. Giles Lt Col. P.D.V.S. VII Corps	26

Army Form C. 2118.

WAR DIARY
INTELLIGENCE SUMMARY.
(Erase heading not required.)

Instructions regarding War Diaries and Intelligence Summaries are contained in F. S. Regs., Part II. and the Staff Manual respectively. Title pages will be prepared in manuscript.

APRIL 1918

Place	Date	Hour	Summary of Events and Information	Remarks and references to Appendices
	April 5th 1918	9:30 am	Sectors move, Capt HILERY for MARTAINVILLE arrived 2 p.m.	Annexed Annexities
	6th		1 BCS ost. Men train came to for parties reported Debion	—
			Don CWS with horse to AHTD ABBEVILLE for transport, 1 Offr & B.O.S. Vety	—
			MHR. Journey 35 Kilometer.	—
	7th		Hoped to bring back horse left on 6th. Rifles Blanks &c. 1 Off & 10 n.h. to	13
			taken to 2 ABOS Horse with Rifles Blanks &c. 1 Off & 10 n.h. to	
			Anvil Mill, to than 12 personnel 2/Lr BWS Offr. 10 delivered 1 Dismount Team	
	8th		Proceeded by road to ABBEVILLE Bannel 1 B.D. 3 h.rs 7/4.	—
	9th		Sectors move 9:30 am Capt. MARTAINEVILLE arrived REGNAUVILLE 7:30 pm (46 kilometers)	—
			owing to darkness billeted for the night. Strength 36 Horses & Pvt H.b. were attacked	
	10th		to W.V.S. on this two days march.	
		7 pm 10h	Left REGNAUVILLE for FAUCQUEMBERGUES arrived 5pm (45 kilometers) Billets by	—
			DADVS to proceed to WAVRANS two long a march for transport horses, billets	
			for the night at AYROULT. Arrived 7 pm. Capt. Cawthra with 1 VCO went	
			on to WAVRANS to select billet. WORCINGHEM nearest billet, poor accommodation.	
	11th	9 am	1 ACO back to AYROULT as guide for Sector personnel. Section moved 8:30 am.	—
			to final billet at PROUY arrived mid-day.	

Army Form C. 2118.

WAR DIARY
INTELLIGENCE SUMMARY.
(Erase heading not required.)

April 1918.

Instructions regarding War Diaries and Intelligence Summaries are contained in F. S. Regs., Part II. and the Staff Manual respectively. Title pages will be prepared in manuscript.

Place	Date	Hour	Summary of Events and Information	Remarks and references to Appendices
PLOUY 15 kilometres SW of ST OMER Sheet 5A	Apl 12/1918.			Animals admitted 4
	13th.		General clean up, horses, saddlery, vehicles etc. Kit inspection by Officer Commanding. Surplus with drawn & deficiencies enquired into. Sections put under one hours notice to move, all vehicles packed, preparations made	2
	14th.	10. am	Ordered by DADVS to move at once, half hour later orders cancelled. 1 Sgt sent to THEROUANNE to take over new billets, reach in by. Evacuated 5 sick animals by road to ST OMER 1 RCD + 29th 1/2 9/C. Mounted Orderly for daily duty with DADVS 16 Div NR	1
	15th.		Letter to Ottawa at VAUDRINGHEM also their new station	3
	16th.		91 CD moved to AIRE mounted orderly. DADVS moved also. Capt Red AVC 2 horses and 2 mules attached to H/ ADS	1
	17th.		1 OR reports from leave at office of DADVS Canada for 6 mths work at Base. Attended sitting foot parade at NICE Xmas. 4 22 control Shot 36 a. (1 Sft + 3 Pte)	2
	18th.		Parade for inspection of Saton offrs. clothing etc. Capt Carter visited Advanced Collecting Post. Orig orders to DADVS. on return from ABBEVILLE delgd inny to move of attest?	1

WAR DIARY or INTELLIGENCE SUMMARY

Army Form C. 2118.

AA14
1918

Place	Date	Hour	Summary of Events and Information	Remarks and references to Appendices
	April 19th/1918		Section left PLOUY 9am for ST MARTIN (AIRE) H22.d.4.2 arrived 1pm.	Originally attached 3
			1 Offr regumes bates from VII Corps V.E.S. Capt Reid AVC with 14th & 8th Bns of 47th R.F.	
			Left at PLOUY for collecting station for rear Corps	
36A H22.d.4.2 ST MARTIN (AIRE)	20th		Sector to Ordnance for Stores. 1 R.O.O. + 1 Ran to LAMBRES and HAMEN ACTON	6
	21st		With Jamnals for rising to units	6
	22nd		1 Offr (attached as skinner) returned to ADVS VII Corps.	1
			Evacuation of 1 anumals (Influenza) to X1 Corps V.E.S. Not loaned for duty	
			With 51st DVS 2pm to 6pm	
	23rd		2 Offrs to GUARBECQUE with 4 mules for issue. 1 Offr to THEROUANNE to Maj G	1
			removed for DHQ. Sender to PLOUY with R.O. Lieut Puigh AVC who took	
			over charge of rear collecting station.	
	24th		1 Offr to HAMBRER to collect 2 - 16h Dn anumals left worth of 2nd Dn V.Q.	4
			Sender to Ordnance for stores	
	25th		Evacuated 3 anumals to X1 Corps V.E.S. Inspection of Section by DDVS First Army	1
	26th		Capt Carter Acting DADVS for Major Devine on leave. 8 Not Loaned to 5th AVC with Major F Jalope, Col Dun P. and Generals. 1 Offr to THEROUANNE to draw stores for D. Sect.	

WJG

Army Form C. 2118.

WAR DIARY
or
INTELLIGENCE SUMMARY.
(Erase heading not required.)

APRIL 1918

Instructions regarding War Diaries and Intelligence Summaries are contained in F. S. Regs., Part II. and the Staff Manual respectively. Title pages will be prepared in manuscript.

Place	Date	Hour	Summary of Events and Information	Remarks and references to Appendices
ST MARTIN (RIRE)	April 27th		M.V.S. detached moved from ROOY to RIPPEMONT. F.S. noted	See 13 F.S. noted
	28th		Completion of repainting and remarking all vehicles	1
	29th		Issued 16 Animals to X1 Corps V.E.S.	3
	30th		Issued 6a 13 Animals do. do.	1

W. Cook (?)
Capt.
Off. Commanding
49th Ave V.S.
16 Mob. Sec.

WAR DIARY / INTELLIGENCE SUMMARY

Army Form C. 2118

MAY 1918

49th Mobile Veterinary Section AVC

Place	Date	Hour	Summary of Events and Information	Remarks and references to Appendices
GENARGEN H.22.d.4.2 36A	May 1/18	9 p/m	Sniper fire of small bore weapons by 1 Eng A.C.D.	2
	2nd		Very few casual wd	4
	3rd		N.C.O. & Men to Base Command. Theatening fire very hvy on outpost by Snipers for 2 hours from E.C. & V.E.S. Mules already on line etc.	8
			Orders to BRESSY to draw lines for 1 Day Col Supp. (on way up camp) Evacuated 10 Animals to XI Corps V.E.S. S/Sjt 1 Farrier CO 9118 attached for treatment	
	4th		(Also?) sick some enemy Post Mortem on mule C.B.118 on-no-1 and H. Anthrax. Carcass skinned and burned	3
	5th		Reg'n to Salvage in Neopha at unserviceable suits	1
	6th		W Captn Arundel worked with 1 Lt Col. Left. Orr & Lorry and of Jucan lorry Presence.	2
	7th		Further to Ordnance for Stores. Shoe Canvas for 45 of XI Corps V.E.S. (2 hours Officer)	-
	8th		Evacuated 6 animals to XI Corps V.E.S.	1
	9th			8
	10th		N.C.O & Men to WITTES to collect 2 animals reported "left without halters" Galloped on 7/5.	1
			Evacuated 7 animals to XI Corps V.E.S.	

Army Form C. 2118.

WAR DIARY
or
INTELLIGENCE SUMMARY.
(Erase heading not required.)

MAY 1916

Place	Date	Hour	Summary of Events and Information	Remarks and references to Appendices
ST OMER	May 11/16		Major Devine DADVS returned from leave. Capt Andrew finished duty of A/DADVS	1
			Wires to Armies/Divs to forward dump of fodder wood	
			Had collected arrival of AVRC no 2 at St OMER BRANCH.	
	12th		Stat. with Return + Pay regards to DGVS mounting not required	2
			2 Res. cart supplement to DGVS (SR) to show extent cases of unusual died ponies/horses	
			Pte to DGVS on first for duty as clerk. Shall utilise Reward to be exercised	
			1st Army Remount THEODORANNE, animals to be evacuated	
	13th		Stock reports Sick animals in Field Park and line from the 39 ½ Army P.	1
	14th			4
	15th		Offer PVO Transferred to DGVS VED reason Infection of personnel of MVSS. Staff Capt now Smyth. Remark No 8 of M/T Hippo and 18 elements AVC	—
	16th		Evacuations animals to ETIVES 1RCD & DOHEM to take over new Rest stations	—
		10am	Lieutn. Coffin DOHEM arrived 3pm Evacuation stores of DWCA arrived under escort	
			Lieut Spiller regained sections from hospital	
	19th	5am	Left DOHEM for WIERRE AU BOIS DIV HQ arrived 3pm (Gen Kavanagh) John Evans St JAMES	3
			MVS detachment HQ from DGVS AVC regained section.	

Army Form C. 2118.

WAR DIARY
INTELLIGENCE SUMMARY.

(Erase heading not required.)

May 1918

Instructions regarding War Diaries and Intelligence Summaries are contained in F. S. Regs., Part II. and the Staff Manual respectively. Title pages will be prepared in manuscript.

Place	Date	Hour	Summary of Events and Information	Remarks and references to Appendices
WIERRE AU BOIS Sh. 12 - S.D. 2.8.	May 18th/1918		Burial Lieut CBH? Knight on (or Lieutenant Colon ?) Burial Conducted by Rev. Cashen	
	19th		Canal of death unknown. Carcass skinned and buried.	
	20th		Sent to Entrance for stores	
	21st	22.00	Went E. REDINGHEM (15 Kilometres) to collect animal left with inhabitant	
	23rd		Went on funeral mind	
			Limber to JAMES for supplies, front to be broken at 4th Brigade	
24th 25th 26th				
	27th		Recvd 2 Horses & Mule on loan) R.L.73 V.P. & Rfts inc. Rep to RM acc for Africa	
	28th		Whne to Collected from D.H.Q on fort and one sect to to 73 V.P. 1 Off. particulars man for home	
	29th		Intn to Ordnance for Stores. Michell provide of 297th LI Regment Reserves trans for met	
	30th		Later returned to section for No to no Lieut. to Last Hq. A.C. (attached)	
	31st		Shot Articles home from D.H.Q. a JAMES	
			1 Pte was toont to his Reg't return to lay in the movement 1st Canadia Divn	

W Moser
Captain
O.C. 67 M.V.S.

Army Form C. 2118.

WAR DIARY
or
INTELLIGENCE SUMMARY.
(Erase heading not required.)

47th Mobile Veterinary Section 16th Div

Vol 30

Place	Date	Hour	Summary of Events and Information	Remarks and references to Appendices
WIERRE AU BOIS Carte 8° 13	June 1st/1918		Usual marching order inspection of Section personnel by D.A.D.V.S.	
	2nd		Limber to Desvres for coal wood	1
	3rd		Limber to Ordnance for Stores	2
			1 V.P/M./1/Sgt. (R/L/Sgt.) Transferred Nominees to No 2 Vety H. authority DVS ltr 24-65/18 35/5/18	
			Limber to Ordnance for Stores. Personnel of 4th Mobile Vety Sec (to American Division) arrived for instruction in duties of a M.V.S. (1 Officer & 20 Other ranks)	1
	4th		Limber to Ordnance for Stores	
	5th		Evacuated 5 animals to No 13 V.P. (wing/foot) Rest on return journey collected animals from LE TURNE. 1 Pte granted 14 days leave	1
	6 & 7th			2
	8th		(Q.M) Stores to LE TURNE. Evacuated animals to No 13 V.P. on arrival at O.B. L. 69.	4
			Evacuated 4 animals to No 13 V.P. one articled on floor from Lonsdale and late one collected on float from LE TURNE	5
	9th		4th American Divisn M.V.S. moved out	1
	10th		Evacuated to No 13 V.P. 3 mules of U.S. Army (wing/foot) Wagon to R.S.P.R. for hot bread	
			Late 8 animals evacuated 2 animals to No 13 V.P. (wing/foot)	1
	11th		Evacd 1 animal wing/foot to 13 V.P. 1 Pte Granted 14 days leave	—

WC

Army Form C. 2118.

WAR DIARY
INTELLIGENCE SUMMARY
(Erase heading not required.)

Place	Date	Hour	Summary of Events and Information	Remarks and references to Appendices
WIERRE AU BOIS	June 12/18	(Camps 13)	Evacuated 1 animal unfitted to No 13 V.H.	Annual Returns
	13th		1 O.R. proceeded 14 days leave.	1
	14th		1 attached Pte sent to Shoot Boys AVC armed & to R.	
			Ruck to Salvage dump and returned with ammunition tables and empties	3
	15th		Harness saddlery inspection	6
			1 O.R. admitted sick to 111th Field Ambulance	
	16th		Wagon to Desvres for Coal wood. 1260 lbs 38cm for prisoners	1
			Limbers to Disinfector for stores	
	17th		Evac'd 13 animals to 13 V[et.] Hosp NEUFCHATEL	13
			Lectures to officers of D.A.D.V.S.	
			for officers & records previous to superseding of D.A.D.V.S. to Sept.	
			Capt Cawthorn acting D.A.D.V.S. of division being temporary absence of Maj Dennis	
	18th		Evac'd 3 animals to No 13 V.H. 1 O.R. sent to 5th C.H.S. attached for duty	3
	19th		1 O.R. returned to duty from 111th Field Ambulance	2
	20th		1 Sgt 1 M.V.S. to inspect all horse lines of unit of Division left us away to look at	
			Sgt Brown AVC dump Camp etc notes of Brigade 46 AVC	1
			Animal C12 R799 sent 2006/pc.cole had lame for Review by Capt Oyster, Comd.	
			Farrier replaced diaphragm Carcase skinned buried	
	21st		1 Driver A.S.C. attached to recover for temporary duty	

W.S.

Army Form C. 2118.

WAR DIARY
INTELLIGENCE SUMMARY.
(Erase heading not required.)

Instructions regarding War Diaries and Intelligence Summaries are contained in F. S. Regs., Part II, and the Staff Manual respectively. Title pages will be prepared in manuscript.

Place	Date	Hour	Summary of Events and Information	Remarks and references to Appendices
WIERRE AU BOIS	June 22nd/1918		Renewed to Ordnance for stores	Private summary
	23rd		Ways to Devres for fuel	—
	24th		Evacuated 16-13 Vdepot Divers	1
	25th		Lieut Cuyh MC 16 Div transferred to No 3 Military Hospital, Number 16	—
	26th		BOULOGNE with the Officers kit	1
	27th & 28th		1 Ote returned from leave, relieved at BOULOG 16 Stays	3
	29th		1 OR proceeded 14 days leave	—
	30th		1 OR returned from leave	2

W. Castellain / Capt
OC 47 MT Cr

2/7/18

WAR DIARY July 1918
INTELLIGENCE SUMMARY
(Erase heading not required.)

Army Form C. 2118.

47th Mobile Veterinary Section

No. 1/8/1918

96C 31

Place	Date	Hour	Summary of Events and Information	Remarks and references to Appendices
WIERRE AU BOIS			CALAIS 13.5.D.3.2.	Animals admitted
	July 1st/1918		Rushes to Ordnance for stores	1
	2nd		Stat 1740 to RE for annual C.B. No. 215	2
	3rd		Stat to ENQUIN HAUT for animal C.B. No. 216	7
	4th		Evacuation by road to R.13 Vety Hp NEUFCHATEL. 10 Horses and 2 Mules. Stat made two journies - C.B. Nos 215 + 217.	1
	5th			1
	6th		Animal CN.16209. Quiet room. Post mortem. Cause of death - Paralysis of Larynx, Oedema.	1
			Remains buried	6
	7.8. 9.10th			3
	11th		O.C. R.C. returns from leave.	1
	12th		Evacuated 9 animals to R13 V.H.	
	13th		Stat to LE TURNE for animal C.B. No 235. Rushes to Ordnance for V.S. Stores.	2
	14th		Rushes to Railhead Buires with In.ch. Veterinary Chest and stores.	2
	15th		Rushes with salvage to SAMER. O.C. R.C. returned from leave	2
	16th - 17th		On Way to BOULOGNE for dental treatment	1

WC

Army Form C. 2118.

WAR DIARY
INTELLIGENCE SUMMARY.

(Erase heading not required.)

47th Mobile Veterinary Section

July 1918

Place	Date	Hour	Summary of Events and Information	Remarks and references to Appendices
WIERRE AU BOIS	July 18th 1918		Evacuated by road to N:13 Veterinary Hospital 9 animals (1 in foal) also three mules	animal destroyed
	19th	10th		1
	20th		Sent to FRENCH to collect animal C13h° 242.	1
	21st		Ellecting to BOULOGNE for dental treatment	1
	22nd		1 Animal (C13h° 243) Evacuated on Float No 13 V.P. Evacuation collected C13h° from SAMER	1
	23rd		2 Animals Evacuated (1 in foal)	1
	24th		2 animals evacuated. 1 line Item sent to war duty station in France	1
	25th, 26th, 27th, 28th, 29th, 30th			2
	31st			

W. Cow Moss
Capt
O. C. 47 Mo V S

Army Form C. 2118.

47th Mobile Veterinary Section
16th Division

WAR DIARY
in AUGUST 1918.

INTELLIGENCE SUMMARY.
(Erase heading not required.)

Instructions regarding War Diaries and Intelligence Summaries are contained in F. S. Regs., Part II. and the Staff Manual respectively. Title pages will be prepared in manuscript.

Place	Date	Hour	Summary of Events and Information	Remarks and references to Appendices
WIERRE AU BOIS S.D.	Aug 1st/1918		Evacuated 8 animals to No 13 V.T.P. Ayrond. Limber to DADVS with office boxes, stationery etc.	2
	2nd		Limber to No 3 Section DAC with veterinary chest. O'Brien	1
	3rd			3
	4th		Shot to HAUT TINGRY for one horse of No 114 Fld A.C. (thrown on Wa LO 13 V.T.P.) Inspection of section animals by DADVS	3
	5th			2
	6th		Shot to DOUDEAUVILLE for sick animal	3
	7th		Sgt Bingley to NIEMBORG to destroy one Sd D animal with fractured leg	13
	8th		1 Pte to 112 Field Ambulance to skin carcase of above destroyed animal. Evacuated 12 animals to No 13 V.T.P. (1 on float). Limber to DESVRES for and invent.	1
	9th			5
	10th		Evacuated 5 animals to No 13 V.T.P.	4
	11th		Limber to Ordnance for Wipes	1
	12th		Limber to Sabrage Dump with "Y" Store	1
	13th			5
	14th		Limber to Ordnance Jordans	2
	15th		Evacuated 13 animals to No 13 V.T.P. (1 on float). 1 N.C.O. & 1 man to disinfect 16th DHQ stables.	4
	16th			4
	17th		Capt Caulkin on France's leave 17/8/18 to 31/8/18. S Pte. R. Carpenter on duty from No 2 C.V.H.O.	4
	18th		1 N.C.O. & 1 man mounted to PONT-Y-BRIDGE to draw 1 Remount fifth Division. Evacuated 16th to No 13 V.T.P. Capt R.H. LAY AVC with 2 servants & horses arrived to take up temporary duty as Officer Commanding. W.E.	13

(A10266) Wt W.5300/P713 750,000 2/18 Sch. 52 Forms/C2118/16.

WAR DIARY
INTELLIGENCE SUMMARY

Army Form C. 2118.

of AUGUST 1918

47th Mobile Veterinary Section
16th Division

Place	Date	Hour	Summary of Events and Information	Remarks and references to Appendices
WIERRE-AU-BOIS	August 14/18		637.6 Cpl Watson A.E. 819 Pte Newton H. 1079 Pte Pue (Boulogne). 3 Other Ranks transferred to 4th Divisional Supply Column ammunition in Exchange for 1 Cpl & 2 Privates to Infantry. Action Notice: left at 3pm for QUEEN arrived 9am - 23 kilometres Divn to remain until further reported again and moves with Divn.	Remarks Omitted
	20th		Remde 3.30am to move same task also new to leave QUEEN 6.30am for 9pm 47 M Vy Sec Camp. Demoyed at MANINGHEM. Arrived 4th 5pm. to MONCHY CAYEUX arrived 9pm. 33k	1
	21st	4 Noon	Ordinary Methods. to BARLIN (16") arrived 11.45pm underlook in billets 57 B 1. N 32 A 7 at K 32 C 3 8 sheet 44 B	1
	22nd	6am	R.A.M.V.T. brushed out. R.4th M.V.T. Capt Munro CAYEUX 6.15am for BARLIN. Remounts party arrived 11.30 am. Remaining to trans part at Rest Bg and arrived BARLIN. 7.30pm. Evacuation Sous-perate Younge	2
BARLIN 44B K.32 B.3.8	23rd	9-D	Lumber to RUITZ on duty for DADVS. Divd Wire and Kitchen Utens 5 10 Coy. ORC. Amm Col 8.8 DADVS 11pm.	6
	24th	9am	Lumber on Parterly for DADVS	
	25th		Lumber to Ordnance for stores. Evacuated 15 animals to R1 V.E.S.	13
	26th		3 men of section to assist. Lumber to Divl Ammunition Stop with M rifles, 1 multifly , box armgar. Projection Evacuated 9 animals to R1 V.E.S. Cap. Lay A.V.C. Prettered 2,43 animals of Divn.	1
	27th		Lumber NOEUX LES MINES for Green Forage on. to Ordnance Stop for rifles. Capt Lay A.V.C. Prettered 56 animals of Division	7
				5

Army Form C. 2118.

WAR DIARY
~~INTELLIGENCE SUMMARY.~~
of AUGUST 1918

(Erase heading not required.)

Instructions regarding War Diaries and Intelligence
Summaries are contained in F. S. Regs., Part II.
and the Staff Manual respectively. Title pages
will be prepared in manuscript.

17th Mobile Veterinary Section
16th Division

Place	Date	Hour	Summary of Events and Information	Remarks and references to Appendices
BARLIN Hut B	Aug 28/17		Went to NOEUX LES MINES for animal cabs. 358. Lent to BEURY with animal for breaking. Antelee Cart by No1. V.E.C. Capt Reg A.V.C. went to Allen to award evidence 135 Reprindes. Animals 7, Detain	5
M32.16.3.6	29th		Rode to NOEUX for pay + forage	4
	30th		Capt Roy evacuated 10th Animal to Duarin	-
	31st		Lecture for and animals + C Roest for pay + forage. Evac. cap. 15 animals CLSF. V.E.C. Capt Reg Veterinary Kennels	11

W Cawthorn
Capt
OC 17 Mob. V.S.

Army Form C. 2118.

WAR DIARY
INTELLIGENCE SUMMARY.
(Erase heading not required.)

47th Mobile Vety Section
16th Div

September 1918

Place	Date	Hour	Summary of Events and Information	Remarks and references to Appendices
BARLIN N.32.c.3.8.				Appendices
	Sept 1st/1918		Capt Cawthorn returned from leave. Links to CAHONNE ROQUART for Rat Capt Lay O/C. Rallied 46 animals of diverse	4.
	2nd		Obs Cpl to Field Ambulance for dressing of elbow (Kicked by horse) Evacuated 14 animals to No 1 V.E.S. Pte Wilson ACC reported 47th O. [indy attached]	11.
	3rd		Links to NOEUX-LES-MINES to draw Green forage. Capt LAY A.V.C. O/O.C. returned to No 3 Dec 16th Dvl. Pte Findlay ACC granted 14 days Special Leave.	3.
	4th		Men to 1.O.M. for repairs. Evacuated 7 animals to No 1 V.E.S.	5.
	5th		Sgt Seary to Field Ambulance for medical examination. Links to VERQUIN for green forage.	1.
	6th		1 O.R. to M.O. for inoculation. Links to Annezin and Annezielle stores. Pte returned from leave.	3.
	7th		Pte King transferred to No 2 V.R. for medical examination for infantry. Links to DROUVIN for green forage. Evacuated 14 animals to No 1 V.E.S.	11.
	8th		1 O.R. to M.O. for inoculation.	8.
	9th		Sgt Seary to Field Ambulance for medical board. Links to for coal wood. Evacuated 22 animals.	20.
	10th		1 O.R. to M.O. for inoculation. Shot repaired, created from 1.O.M. workshop R.H.7.2 Links to DROUVIN for Green forage.	1.
	11th			2.

WAR DIARY or INTELLIGENCE SUMMARY.

Army Form C. 2118.

49th Mobile Veterinary Section

Sep/1918

Place	Date	Hour	Summary of Events and Information	Remarks and references to Appendices
BERLIN Sept	12/1918		Links to HOUDAIN for grain forage. Pte Burton granted one months leave on Draft. 1 O.R. to M.O. for inoculation. Evacuated animals No 1/6 S. as un-serviceable.	5.
	13th	2.30pm	Inspection by Divisional General Army Veterinary Corps	
	14th		1 O.R. to M.O. for inoculation. Links to HERSIN COUPIGNY & HOUDAIN for Cosh Evacuated animals to HOUDAIN for animal No 10 + 58 T.M.V.E.S.	2.
	15th		Sgt Soopy admitted to Field Ambulance + Evacuated	5.
	16th		1 O.R. to M.O. for inoculation. Links to Rocking Coal Evacuated animals to No 1/6 S	9.
	17th		1 R.S.O. rode down to see at Horse Dep (Dangu) report 32 unable of service with Field Force. Horse Branch announcing to 67 want kit water + Field used Cart returned.	1.
	18th		1 O.R. to M.O. for inoculation. This being section percentage up to 100.	2.
	19th		Links to D.A.C. for repair. Horse to D.A.C. for CB no 74. Evacuated animals to 6 R.V.N.E.S. 1 O.R. opened section from N 12/6 S ground used for grazing.	1.
	20th		Links repairs collected from 142 CRE.	1.
	21st		1 O.R. to leave to DROUVIN to take over M.V.S. Field in our area	2.
	22nd		1 O.R. started 14 days leave	2.
	23rd		Section Horse. Left BARLIN 10.10am for DROUVIN. Splinter arrived 11.15am Had repairs new field. Lt. C.S.L. Foot 4th B. Restablished to BARLIN for Annual C.P.H. 4th. Destroyed case unable to walk. One animal admitted 2nd hole. Covers Strained Bones	2.

W.G.

WAR DIARY / INTELLIGENCE SUMMARY

Army Form C. 2118.

47th Mobile Vety Sectn
19th Divn

Sep 1/1918

Place	Date	Hour	Summary of Events and Information	Remarks and references to Appendices
DROUVIN Km.O.S.T.	Sep 24/1918		Float sent for repairs to 111th Field Ambulance reported sick, admitted, evacuated to No 6 C.C.S. 1 Driver returned from leave. Horse teams with lorries for removal of manure	Animals Admitted 1
	25th		Wagon to D.A.D.V.S. for 1 load of corrugated iron. 2 men with horse and cart removed 5 loads of manure from inhabitant (farmer) to assist in keeping billet. Brazier's admitted to 5/9 V.E.C. BROWN	3
	26th		Lorries to NOEUX for 1 load of hay for horse standings. Several horses develop cases of Anaemia, to be admitted to section for cure. Vitamin'd. 3 Dun of Artillery to assist.	2
	27th		Lorries to NOEUX for 1 load hay. Clipping of section animals completed.	1
	28th		Wagon to BEAUVRY for 1st load of oats. Lorries to BOULOGNE for coal wood and to HOUCHIN for potatoes. 10 men with French Cart removed 10 loads manure	2
	29th		80 remount horses were issued to units of Division. 1 Cpl & 1 Pte P.C.C. proceeding on leave. 1 Sgt reported for duty when for relief duty for Sgt A/C to complete establishment of section.	1
	30th		Evacuated 4 animals to 9 V.E.S. Float repaired returned from Divn. Wagon to BEAUVRY for one of oats. Lumber to R.E. at SAILLY LABOURSE for stores. Cart to VERQUIN for oats for indicator.	2

W. Moore
Capt M.C.
O.C. 47 MVS

Army Form C. 2118.

21 October 1918. WAR DIARY or INTELLIGENCE SUMMARY.

(Erase heading not required.)

Place	Date	Hour	Summary of Events and Information	Remarks and references to Appendices
PROUVIN Sheet 44B K.4.c.5.7.	1st	9.10a	Lt/Col Winckley granted leave to U.K. 2.10.18 to 16.10.18 via CALAIS. Limber to VERQUIN for coal. Wagon to NEUX-LES-MINES for slag. Limber to Salvage dump for remaining material, went for chaff.	Animals admitted 2
"	2nd		Wagon + loader to BEUVRY for water. Limber to 46th Heavy Artillery Brigade for horse for animal. Limber to HOUCHIN B144 B4z REA	4
	3rd		Limber to NEUX-LES-MINES for stores. Also 4 Judas 4 horses 2 mules. Limber evacuated to WIVES dust with two animals to WIVES. Lt/Col Blackburn to NEUX-LES-MINES for butcher	6
	4th		Advanced post opened at ANNEQUIN. Lt/Col Blackburn + 3 men mounted post with stores to ANNEQUIN. About to CAMBRIN for 1 hr.1 x stores to butcher.	5
	5th		Limber to BARLIN for coal. Pte Lucas with water cart to advanced post. Pte Mackie returned to Section from advanced post.	2
	6th		Limber to Advanced post with rations + brought back load of slag. Pte Mackie granted leave to U.K. 7.10.18 to 31.10.18	1

Army Form C. 2118.

WAR DIARY
or
INTELLIGENCE SUMMARY.
(Erase heading not required.)

Instructions regarding War Diaries and Intelligence Summaries are contained in F. S. Regs., Part II. and the Staff Manual respectively. Title pages will be prepared in manuscript.

October 1918

Place	Date	Hour	Summary of Events and Information	Remarks and references to Appendices
DROUVIN Huts 4.B K4.c.5.7.	7.10.18			
	8th		Evacuated 8 horses to No 1 V.E.S. 2 float users. Admitted from advances post 4 horses 2 mules. Discharged 2 horses to Div 713rd R.F.A.	Arrivals Admissions 4
	9th		Similar to advanced post with return. Sgt Taylor returned from leave. Sgt dept horse went to advanced post. Pte Blackburn returned to section from advanced post.	1
	10th		Similar to Cadamanes. Float to No 1 V.E.S. Evacuated 4 animals to 1 V.E.S. Admitted 3 horses 1 mule from advanced post.	4
	11th		Similar to advanced post with iron for building bridges also load of hay. Admitted from advanced post 3 horses 1 mule. Lieut. Brennie? changed dietpod for Lieut. took D.A.D.V.S. durable.	5
	12th		Wagon to advanced post with supplies on 1 lorry ft truck layer store. Similar to DARLIN for coal. Evacuated 2 horses 2 mules to No 1 V.E.S.	1
	13th		Nil to Cadamanes.	1

WAR DIARY / INTELLIGENCE SUMMARY

October 1918.

Army Form C. 2118.

Place	Date	Hour	Summary of Events and Information	Remarks and references to Appendices
DROUVIN Sheet 44 I.4.c.5.4	14.10.18		About to W.I.D.A.C. to Proceed for mules also to 116th Div. Agricultural Company for horses. Wagon to advanced post with wood and returned with load of slag.	Ammunition detachment 5
	15th		About to W. I.V.E.S. to assist in Evacuating horses.	6
ANNEQUIN	16th		Section moved to ANNEQUIN, starting at 10.30, arriving at 11.00. Evacuated 10 horses + 3 mules to W. I.V.E.S. About to 130 Bde. R.F.A. + D 144 Bde. R.F.A. for 2 horses. Limber to DROUVIN for stores left behind. 3 hides sent to W.I.V.E.S. Advanced Mobile Detachment moved to HAINES.	13
	17th		About to advanced limber collecting post (times). Sent to B180/136 R.F.A. for animal limber to Divisional Stores SAILLY-LABOURSE with "Lüblenz's" 5 Auto grinders. Limber to DROUVIN for spare forage machine	4
BERCLEAU	18th		Section moved to BERCLEAU starting at 11.30 + arriving at 14.00. Ambulance collected 2 sick animals + took them to W. I.V.E.S.	1
PHALEMPIN	19th		Section moved to PHALEMPIN, starting at 11.00 + arriving at 16.00. Lft. Winkley returned from leave.	2

WAR DIARY
INTELLIGENCE SUMMARY

October 1918

Army Form C. 2118.

Place	Date	Hour	Summary of Events and Information	Remarks and references to Appendices
TEMPLEUVE.	20.10.18		Section moved to TEMPLEUVE, starting at 09.00 + arriving at 13.00. Cpl Stephens rejoined Section from 44th Bde Infantry Immediate. CRS 564 + 568 left M.R.F. N° 1 at FELICIE LABBE RUE DES OUVELETTES PHALEMPIN.	Animals submitted 3
	21st		D.A.D.V.S. returned from leave. Cpl. Cawthorn finished duty of A/D.A.D.V.S. S/M Fisher granted 14 days leave to U.K. 23.10.18 to 6.11.18	5
	22nd		Cpl Winkley to D.A.D.V.S. office for clerical work.	1
LA-POSTERIE Sheet 44 A.5.d 8.6	23rd		Section moved to LA-POSTERIE starting at 15.00 + arriving at 17.30. Cpl Blackburn + 1 man left at TEMPLEUVE as Detachment.	3
	24th		Limber to TEMPLEUVE with rations for Detachment. Pte Mackie returned from leave. Cpl Hoffmeur to collect CRS 581 at TAINTIGNIES. Flood to collect CRS 580 at ROUMES.	2
	25th		Cart to Detachment with rations, also assisted civilians to TEMPLEUVE. Flood to collect animal CRS 583 from C Bty 180 Bde RFA at TAINTIGNIES. Cart to TEMPLEUVE with CRS 580	2
	26th		Cart to detachment at TEMPLEUVE with CRS.W. 581.583 Cart to detachment with rations	6

WAR DIARY
or INTELLIGENCE SUMMARY

Army Form C. 2118.

Instructions regarding War Diaries and Intelligence Summaries are contained in F.S. Regs., Part II. and the Staff Manual respectively. Title pages will be prepared in manuscript.

October 1918   1-11-18

(Erase heading not required.)

Place	Date	Hour	Summary of Events and Information	Remarks and references to Appendices
LA POSTERIE Sheet 44 A 5.d.8.6.	27.10.18		Left with rations for detachment at TEMPLEUVE	Animals Submitted
	28th		Went to RUMES for animal CB. 600 from "C" Bty 180 Bde RFA. Left with rations to detachment at TEMPLEUVE. Evacuated 14 animals to M⁰ I.V.E.S. 1 Sgt 1 offr/lr & 1 2 Bdr	8
	29th		Went with rations to detachment at TEMPLEUVE. Evacuating party returned.	4
	30th		Left with rations to detachment at TEMPLEUVE. Two mounted men to TEMPLEUVE from detachment went to TAINTIGNIES to collect 5 animals CB 602·603·604 Wagon for hay. Left to TEMPLEUVE. 1 black gelding #RF22 CyR. 105 Bus. F. & Lux TAINTIGNIES	2
	31st		Left with rations to detachment at TEMPLEUVE also to call at Divisional dump for Brewers grindles. Went to TAINTIGNIES for CB 609 D Bty 180 Bde. Wagon for hay.	1

W. Barr Capt
O.C. 4th M.V.S.

WAR DIARY / INTELLIGENCE SUMMARY

Army Form C. 2118.

NOVEMBER 1918

49th Mobile Vety Section

Place	Date	Hour	Summary of Events and Information	Remarks and references to Appendices
La Posterie Hut 91 R.S.d.8.6. Sh.44	1918 1st		First line transport to BACHY. to draw rations forage. Cart with rations for detached party at TEMPLEUVE and for Divisional Stores. In billets at TEMPLEUVE.	2
	2nd		Rations forage sent to detachment. Own transport to BACHY for supplies. Evacuated 4 animals 47 V.E.S. (including 1 flat case) AVERN	1
	3rd		Own transport for rations. Float to TEMPLEUVE with animal for detachment	1
	4th		First line transport to draw supplies from BACHY, daily to 9th instant. Cart with rations to TEMPLEUVE and for Ordnance Stores	1
	5th		2 animals evacuated per motor ambulance	1
	6th		Cart with rations for detachment and to Forage dump with "M" Clothing 3/6	10
	7th		Limber to CRE TEMPLEUVE for building material for station	2
	8th		Float collected animal from TEMPLEUVE. Cart to TEMPLEUVE with rations	1
	9th		Float collected animal from RUMES. 1 Pte returned from leave	2
	10th		Section moved to RUMES 7.29.C.2.4. Shu 37 Evacuated 9 animals to 47 V.E.S. TEMPLEUVE. Detachment rejoined section.	1
	11th		Float collected one animal RUMES	4
	12th		Evacuated 4 animals to 4.7.9. V.E.S. TEMPLEUVE. 1 Cpl rejoined section from 16 D.V.Q. (DADVS's office)	7

Army Form C. 2118.

WAR DIARY
INTELLIGENCE SUMMARY.

(Erase heading not required.)

49th Mobile Veterinary Section
16th Division

NOVEMBER 1916

Instructions regarding War Diaries and Intelligence Summaries are contained in F. S. Regs., Part II. and the Staff Manual respectively. Title pages will be prepared in manuscript.

Place	Date	Hour	Summary of Events and Information	Remarks and references to Appendices
ROPES T.29.c.2.4 Sheet 57.	13/11/16		Evacuated 7 animals to No 7 V.E.S.	Animals admitted 3.
	14th		Horse-clocked animal from WEZ-MACAIN.	1
			Evacuated 1 animal to No 7 V.E.S. Lister worked. Painted.	
	15th		One Pte granted 14 days leave. Evacuated 11 animals to No 7 V.E.S. including 1 Lst 4 Bn to ENNEVELIN to take over new billet.	8
ENNEVELIN F.8.a.9.9. Sheet 44a.	16th	9.30am	Section moved from ROPES to ENNEVELIN arrived 11.15am. 1 attached all Drum. parked 14 days leave.	1
	17th		Limber to PHALEMPIN for Ice.	1
	18th		1 Pte + 1 Smith granted 14 days leave.	2
	19th		Vehicles washed, ready for repainting	1
	20th		First line transport to draw rations daily. (ENNEVELIN Dump)	1
	21st		1 Sgt to HQ 49th Inf Bde for temp duty as acting Sgt (relief) Wagon to LA POSTE DE JOR. Beaucho Hink and to ATTICHES for Ordnance Stores	2
	22nd		1 Cpl granted 14 days leave 2 Horse Clipping machines since returned to Infantry Bdes	5
	23rd		Evacuated 7 animals to No 7 V.E.S. at LA POSTERIE. Wagon to ATTICHES for ordnance Stores. Riding Horses loaned to Villers Hy for Bde.	1
	24th		1 Cpl transferred to No 32 Vety Hospl for training and GHQ AVC to a field Unit.	1

Army Form C. 2118.

WAR DIARY
or
INTELLIGENCE SUMMARY.
(Erase heading not required.)

47th Mobile Vety Section
16th Division

Instructions regarding War Diaries and Intelligence Summaries are contained in F. S. Regs., Part II. and the Staff Manual respectively. Title pages will be prepared in manuscript.

Month November 1918.

Place	Date	Hour	Summary of Events and Information	Remarks and references to Appendices
ENNEVELIN F.B.Q.9.9. Sheet 37.	25/11/18		Wagon to Ordnance for stores.	Animals Admitted
	26th		1 Pte to Hd Qr 47th Sect for temp duty as Sgt A.V.C. being Sgt in hospital. 1 Pte granted 10 days leave to CHANTILLY, FRANCE. 1 Pte granted 14 days leave to UK	1
	27th		Evacuated 7 animals to No 29. V.E.S. at LA BRETRIE. Wagon to PONT-A-MARCQ for two loads of timber.	2
	28th		Wagon to Ordnance for stores. (Attached)	1
	29th		Rations forage to be drawn from PONT-A-MARCQ, daily by first line transport. Capt Burton and Sgt Taylor to MONS-EN-PEVELES and visited a suitable site for section.	1
	30th		Party of 1 Cpl & 6 O. Rks Arthur collected rubbish between TEMPLEUVE and PONT-A-MARCQ for section.	1

W. Lew Morr
Captain A.V.C.
O.C. 47th M.V.S.

Army Form C. 2118.

47th Mobile Veterinary Section. 1/6th Div.

WAR DIARY
INTELLIGENCE SUMMARY.
(Erase heading not required.)

Place	Date	Hour	Summary of Events and Information	Remarks and references to Appendices
CANCHOMPRE 2 F.2.1.a.4.2 Sheet 44 A.	Feb. 1st 1918		Section moved 2pm to FERME DE CANCHOMPRER. one hours march.	1 Animal admitted
	2nd		Boot sent to 2am TEMPLEUVE. Limber to PONT A MARCQ for fuel. 1 Sgt returned from HdQrs 49th Inf Bde (detached duty)	2.
	3rd		2 Draught Horses loaned to farmer for day.	2.
	4th		1 Rider for trap and 3 horses for draught loaned to farmer. Cart with Riding Horse loaned to A.D.V.S. 2 Ptes returned from leave. Wagon to AVELIN for ordnance stores and to ATTICHES for R.E. Stores	2.
	5th		Evacuated 7 animals to 47 V.E.S. Horse (cart loaned to farmer for day) 1 Pte returned from HdQrs 49th Inf Bde. (relief duty)	3
	6th		Horse 'Cart loaned to farmer for day. 3 Draught Horses returned from leave. Wagon to PONT-A-MARCQ for fuel.	13
	7th		3 Draught Horses loaned to farmer for day. Evacuated 25 animals to 47 V.E.S. Wagon to DOUBRES with one load of hay.	9.
	8th		Horse 'Cart loaned to farmer for day. 1 Pte returned from leave. 1 Pte joined Section for duty from 2/4 V.A.P. Explosion shell 8.30pm on PONT-A-MARCQ road. 2 Horses of D/180 Bde R.F.A. destroyed by order of Capt Authon.	4.
	9th		Wagon to AVELIN for ordnance stores. 3 Draught Horses loaned to farmer. 1 Cpl returned from leave. Wagon Horses loaned to farmer for removal of manure.	8.

WAR DIARY

INTELLIGENCE SUMMARY.

(Erase heading not required.)

Army Form C. 2118.

17th MOBILE SECTION
No. December 1918.

Place	Date	Hour	Summary of Events and Information	Remarks and references to Appendices
F.21.a.H.2. Sheet 44A	Dec 10/18		2 Horses loaned to farmer for day and 2 for halfday	Animals Returned 1.
	11th		1 Sgt granted 14 days leave to U.K. 1 horse Cart loaned to farmer for day. 1 Pte (Cal.Ariver) to Orientation Camp for demobilisation. Float returned and collected from Don. TEMPLEUVE. Float collected animal from WACHEMY & EUUEVELIN 13 animals to 727.V.E.S. and took on to 727.V.E.S. wagon for two loads of old tanks	2.
	12th		10 Horses to TOURMIGNIES for examination as brood mares. 1 Draught horse loaned to farmer. wagon for 1 load of old tanks. 1 Pte returned from leave. 1 Pte to NOR H17 Sgf Pte Temp duty as Sgt. Driver	5.
	13th		Cart to TEMPLEUVE for R.S. Ackries	4.
	14th		Cart to TEMPLEUVE for cooking over from R.S. Workshop. Evacuated 8 animals to 727.V.E.S.	1.
	15th		1 Pte to NOR H8 Sgf Pte Temp duty as Sgt. Driver. 1 Pte returned from leave.	-
	16th		Horse Cart loaned to farmer. halfday 3 Draught horse loaned to farmer halfday. Float pair horses loaned to farmer for halfday.	16.
	17th		Wagon to AVELIN for ordnance stores and to ENNEVELIN for old boiler, for melting of mange dressing. 1 Draught horse loaned to farmer for halfday.	6.
	18th		1 Pte to DHR, temp duty as groom for S.A.D.V.S. 2 Draught horses loaned to farmer for day	2.
	19th		Evacuated 22 (illegible) 727.V.E.S. Float with 5 mules. 1 Horse loaned to farmer for day	4.

Army Form C. 2118.

WAR DIARY
INTELLIGENCE SUMMARY.
(Erase heading not required.)

47th MOBILE SECTION, A.V.C.
December 1918

Place	Date	Hour	Summary of Events and Information	Remarks and references to Appendices
F.21.a.4.2.				Appendices Admitted
	Dec 20/1918		1 Draught horse loaned to farmer for day, 1 Pte returned from No. 47 M.S. 1 wagon to AVELIN for ordnance stores and to ATTICHES for building materials	2
	21st		Limber to PONT A MARCQ for fuel. 3 Draught horses loaned to farmer for daily work. Cart to ATTICHES for building materials.	15
	22nd Dec 23rd		3 Hrs. Cart loaned to farmer for day. Transfer 1 animals to No. 27 V.E.S. Animal C/13741 died. Post mortem - Cause of death Colicus. Corpse skinned & buried	5
	24th		Dust line transport drew rations & forage for two days, wagon to ATTICHES for R.E. stores. 1 Pte returned from 2 No. leave	3
	25th Xmas Day		INSPECTION by DDVS 1st Army & ADVS 1st Corps.	5½
	26th & 27th		Limber to PONT A MARCQ for fuel	1
	28th		Evacuated 9 animals to No. 1 V.E.S. Gloss arm with hostilities	3
	29th		1 Sgt returned from leave	2
	30th		Limber to AVELIN for ordnance stores. Escort to DISTRICT COURT for animal C/BR. 785	5
	31st		1 Pte reported for duty from 2nd V.R. to complete establishment. One draught horse loaned to farmer for day	37

W. Claud Morse
Capt. R.A.V.C.
O.C. 47 M.V.S.
2/1/1919.

WAR DIARY / INTELLIGENCE SUMMARY

Army Form C. 2118.

49th Mobile Veterinary Section
16th Division

January 1919.

Place	Date	Hour	Summary of Events and Information	Remarks and references to Appendices
FRETIN DE CAMPHIN-PEVÈLE F.21.a.A.2	Jan 1st/1919		Evacuated #3 animals to 2. 1. V.E.S. including one foot case.	1.
	2nd		Wagon to PITCHES for Ordnance Stores. 10th returned to Base from 14th H.S. Inf. Bde.	32.
	3rd		Cast collected sick animal from OSTRICOURT. Limber to PONT-à-MARCQ & Forfret. One extra draught horse loaned to farmer for day, other 3 animals loaned for road duty.	137.
	4th		Evacuated #5 animals to 2. 1. V.E.S. including one foot case.	1.
	5-6th		1 Draught horse, extra loaned to farmer for day with driver	6
	7th		Wagon to make two journies daily for stabling forage.	11
	8th		Evacuated 12 animals to R. 1. V.E.S. including one on float.	3.
	9th		Horse Cart loaned to farmer for day. Float to Ostrichon at TEMPLEUVE with	18
	10th		animal for slaughter. (Fracture Tibia) Evacuated 9 animals to 2.1 V.E.S. Wagon to Pont a Marcq for Mail. 10th marched 14 day leave. Limber to 1.C.M. Iron plane with float wheels for repair. Animal (C.B.R.? D.W.) for Parkin by Capt Ashton. — calculus and rupture bladder, carcase returned received. Brooks Corbie of Veterinary Instruction commenced at 49 A.V.C. for R.C.O.S men of units of 16th Division. 3 R.C.O.S men reported for course, 3 Lectures weekly by all Veterinary Officers of Division. Daily Instruction by Lt. Sylvester R.A.V.C.	17
	11th & 12th		Wagon to Ordnance for leave.	1.
	13th		Limber to TEMPLEUVE for R.E. Stores. Wagon to PONT a MARCQ for Mail. 10th granted 14 days leave.	10.

Army Form C. 2118.

47 Mobile Veterinary Section
16 Div

WAR DIARY
INTELLIGENCE SUMMARY.

JANUARY 1919 (Erase heading not required.)

Instructions regarding War Diaries and Intelligence Summaries are contained in F. S. Regs., Part II. and the Staff Manual respectively. Title pages will be prepared in manuscript.

47th MOBILE SECTION. A.V.C.
No. M/1033
Date 2/2/19

Place	Date	Hour	Summary of Events and Information	Remarks and references to Appendices
January	14th/1919		D.D.V.S. 1st Army inspected animals for sale, passed 126 to be sold. Animals remitted.	3.
	15th/16th		by auction at PONT-A-MARCQ on 22nd inst. Wagon to SOM. TEMPLEUVE for repairs, one borrowed from 14.26 R.A.C.C. ENNEVELIN	9.
	17th		Cart to ATICHES for ordnance stores. Stables to PONT-A-MARCQ for fuel.	6.
	18th		Evacuated 29 animals to No. 1 V.E.S.	1.
	19th		126 animals taken to be premises at PONT-A-MARCQ.	
	20 & 21st		for duty of grooming, hand clipping & table branding. Limited to ATICHES for ordnance stores.	3
	22nd		126 animals sold by auction at PONT-A-MARCQ.	3
	23 & 24th		Wagon to PONT-A-MARCQ for fuel.	10.
	25th		Evacuated 15 animals to No.1 V.E.S.	1
	26 & 27th		Animal C13 No.89 Destroyed (fractured tibia) taken to butcher at TEMPLEUVE for fleet	3
	28 & 29th		Evacuated 26 animals to No.1 V.E.S.	23.
	30 & 31st		Wagon to PONT-A-MARCQ for fuel.	6.

W G au Noel
Captain R.A.V.C.
O.C. 47 M.V.S.

Feb 2nd/1919.

WAR DIARY / INTELLIGENCE SUMMARY

Army Form C. 2118.

47th MOBILE SECTION A.V.C.

Month: February 1919

Place	Date	Hour	Summary of Events and Information	Remarks and references to Appendices
FERME-DE-CANCHOMPREZ F.21.a.4.2 Sheet II a.	Feb 1/1919		Wagon repair collected from I.O.M. TEMPLEUVE. Veterinary Course at 47 M.V.T. completed, personnel returned to units.	1
	2nd	13:00	Sgt & 2 men to PONT A MARCQ. to put shelters over pits & drain of 133 animals from 2"DRs for public auction on 3rd.	6
	4th 5th		Wagon made two journeys for native forage. Part of sale gone PONT A MARCQ.	21
	6th		Capt Arthur Premier 13 days leave. 2 OR's to 5 H.V.E.S. for 2 WVS	—
	7th		Wagon to PONT A MARCQ. Premier 13 days leave.	2
	8th		An Maren Jr. chapeau to England. 2 O.R. to 1st Can REC at THUMESNIL to Unite.	12
	9th 10th		Premier D.N°1 V.E.S. 17 days chapeau to England.	—
	11th 12th 13th		OR's returned from leave, leave extended by W.O. from 22/1/19 to 7/2/19. Wagon employed as trains, no extra movement of 1 pm native addresses a wag. begun for and Ole Stanley returned from leave to be accompanied by W.O. 39/1 to 1/3 and to 15/1/19. Premier 20 36 animals to 5 Mob V.E.S. receiving two Fast Cases	10
			1 animal evacuated by No1 TEMPLEUVE.	
	14th		1 A.D.V.S. 1st Corps inspected Section & wagons to BIRMANQUE & guides.	2
		6 pm	Maj ch ALELIN (DADVS) for disposal hand of section to D.D.V.S. 1st Corps at CYSOING	
	15th		Evacuated 6 animals to 5 Mob V.E.S. OR return to WATTIGNIES with one D mule returned to I.O.M. Corps base Dept. 2 R.A. to TEMPLEUVE with one mule. 113 Field Ambulance 4 one O.D. for 140 Artillery Res. inquire for Winter to Dept.	2
	16th 17th		1 Cpl with R.E. to Rlwl unit & 2 minch to Ill aupen; Major Lindegman arranged for 17 pokets & information to meet E.S.B.	1

47 Mobile Veterinary Section 15 Div
9/8 39

WAR DIARY
or
INTELLIGENCE SUMMARY.
(Erase heading not required.)

Army Form C. 2118.

47th MOBILE SECTION A.V.C.
No. M/136
Date 2/3/19

47th Mobile Veterinary Section
15 Div

Instructions regarding War Diaries and Intelligence Summaries are contained in F. S. Regs., Part II. and the Staff Manual respectively. Title pages will be prepared in manuscript.

Place	Date	Hour	Summary of Events and Information	Remarks and references to Appendices
	Feb 18/19		Gave to F.O.E.T.N. for animal C.A.S. 191. Wagon to A.V.E.I.N. for Mane Vac attn. Note	Print 2 Armed 2
			for ration. W.A.S. reposing.	
	19th		Remained 5 animals to 27th V.E.S.	1
			Daily fur dressing above proper.	
	20th		O.R. Boven to Litani. 112nd Field Ambulance. O.R. Row Holland at 113 Field Ambulance.	
			A.V.E.I.N. for supply handing approved of thrown sleeves for sale. wag + x-2 min.	
			to take Jack Down to Messo for future duty	22
	21st		Issued the 64 V.E.S. with animals for slaughter. Wagon to Phil-hospital. 10 animals	
			of Downs sold by Auctr at Pontamaroca.	2
	21nd		Evacuated 23 animals to 27th V.E.S. Cpl Cotton returned from leave	-
	23rd		O.R. Nadus admitted to 112nd Fd Ambulance. Wagon to Aegysta for animal flour	-
	25th Feb	2 A.M.	Number to A.V.E.I.N. for 10000 hand plaits. O.R. Ans Grover 1st Battalion Cnr Holton W.	13
			Bologne with Vector dog for shipment to England via B.E.D. 14157 + Bnas Ruttly.	
	26th		Evacuated 13 animals to 27th V.E.S. Lt. Cpl than to prepare 12 Promises at	-
			Pontamaroca. O.R. Chipperd returns from leave	
	27th		Lamba to take gard with pope thunder shoes. (3 Animals admitted, Numbered strained	-
	27th		An additional 48 animals admitted for sale in hands 1 or (Numbered shandet)	-
			W Bradbury	

W Gans Waver
Captain R.A.V.C
O.C. 47 M.V.S.

Army Form C. 2118.

47th MOBILE SECTION A.V.C.
No. M/1341
Date 2/4/19

WAR DIARY

INTELLIGENCE SUMMARY

Month MARCH 1919

Place	Date	Hour	Summary of Events and Information	Remarks and references to Appendices
FERME DE CANCHOMPREZ TEMPLEUVE (NORD) Ref 4/11/19	1st		148. Class "2" (surplus) animals sold by auction at PONT A MARCQ.	Animals remitted Rem. 1. MAP MARCQ
	2nd		One Private granted 14 days leave. Wagon to PONT-A-MARCQ for fuel.	1.
	3rd		Stat to MONS-EN-PEVELE for animal CB No 231. Remitted orderly for F.D.V.S. 1st Echa. 1 A.D. Horse, shoe "By" sent to BERJEE en route for England.	1. 5.
	4th 5th		Evacuated 12 animals to N° 1 V.E.S. mobiling 1 float 2012	6.
	6th		Sgt. Cpl. with cart to MONS-EN-PEVELE to prepare premises for sale of animals 150. Wagon with rations forage for sale personnel Lammas. 1 Dsm. DIEGO N° 142262 for death by fatigue 4 days late	4.
	7th		Wagon to Pont a Marcq with rations forage. Stat to MATTIGNIES for animal GB 2,173	4.
	8th		Evacuated 8 animals to N° 1 V.E.S. mobiling 1 invalid. Wagon to MONS-EN-PEVELE for sale of stores.	Dec.
9th to 10th			Sgt. Cpl. & Pte to PONT A MARCQ & MONS. Sets up premises for sale of animals on 13th and 15th	N° 789 Dec. 3.
	11th		Wagon with rations forage to PONT A MARCQ. 2 Dvs. PRICE (MELTON & WHEATLEY) transferred to N° 9 V.E.S. attending 9% RARC (MELTON & WHEATLEY) transferred to 16 detls 043 RARC Base Base 76/11/8/19. Personnel of water bowser 16 detls 043. 150 animals for sale admitted at PONT A MARCQ Stat collected animal GB 2,176 from MATTIGNIES	3. 3.
	12th		1 section Rider transferred to 108 any ASC R.D. Wagon to PONT A MARCQ division forage. Cart to AVELIN with returned advance stores. Evacuated 1 animal to N° 7 V.E.S. mobiling 1 flat card	4,150 Dec. 2
	13th		150 animals sold by auction at PONT A MARCQ. Wagon with rations forage. Cart to remove stores to MONS for sale. 150 animals admitted	2,150 Bcd.
	14th		Wagon to MONS with rations. Stat to WATTIGNIES for sale and animal of C/100. Wagon to Pau & tray for fuel	2.
	15th		150 animals sold by auction at MONS EN PEVELE. Evacuated 17 animals 8 N° 1 V.E.S. (invalid)	17. Soil 4,150 Soil
16th 17th			Evacuated 9 animals to N° 9 V.E.S. 2 Drs refined from leave	2.
	18th		Stat to TEMPLEUVE for animal C/8291. One Rider (5m.) of 2nd DVP 16 Br. and N° 9 V.E.S. for England	5.
	19th		Evac 7 animals to N° 9 V.E.S.	-
20th 21st			Rations forage delivered by motor lorry. Wagon from & horses loaned. Two fatts. ambulance dog S. section Riders to Rider of Rule & Supplies sent to ROUEN	
	22nd		Wagon from Forage Depot 51 N° 712 Field Ambulance for day. Cut with ambulance 1.C.S.	3.
			Evacuated 4 animals to N° 9 V.E.S. at TEMPLEUVE	3.

Army Form C. 2118.

WAR DIARY
MARCH 1919
INTELLIGENCE SUMMARY.

47th Mobile Veterinary Section
(6 Div.)

47th MOBILE SECTION, A.V.C.
No. W/1341
2/4/19

Place	Date	Hour	Summary of Events and Information	Remarks and references to Appendices
	23/3/19		Mob. Equipment sorted & checked for inspection, Major New issued #712 Stalebeace horses	forward Admitted
	24"		Wagon 13 D.C.S. Templeuve with "U" + 8" Divs. Surplus Bran still retained "Gratin Dump?"	1
	25"		By Taylor & RR Mackie to Convalescent C of R for demobilization. Passed 143 LD. Horses of Destin. grade "Y" to DOUAI en route for England	6
	26"		By Coffeeire Rare #113 Batty Ambulance to Infermed Revocation of Horses + Ridley. Evacuated 7 animals to No. 1 V.E.S.	2
	27"		Wagon to Templeuve I.O.S. with "U" + 8" Divs.	1
	28"		Awaiting orders for demobilization & relieve Section to Cadre A	1
	29"/30/31		Orders to be transferred to Personnel Bran dump, personnel of Cadre A to be transferred to 144 Co R.A.S.C.	1

W. Bew Moor
Capt. R.A.V.C.
O.C. 47 M.V.S.

April 1919
missing

WAR DIARY / INTELLIGENCE SUMMARY

Army Form C. 2118.

May 1919
47 Mobile Veterinary Section
R 1 Area

Place	Date	Hour	Summary of Events and Information	Remarks and references to Appendices
St Saulve VALENCIENNES	1/5/19		Lectim Marianens posted to this unit. Came to be attached vice two personnel for the formation of a newly reconstituted M.V.Sn on clearing up work in R.1 Area. Animals to offices of D.D.V.S for duty.	Animals Admitted /Remarks
	2nd 3rd		General duties	1
	4th		Motor Ambulance to YPRES MARQUILLIES taking ten [?] horses with P.C.J. to be exchanged. Unobtainable [?]. Horse that to attend animal from R.1 Area. Valence R.V.C. Animal had been destroyed. Park mortem examination by CAV[?].	1
			General Admissions stables	
	5th		Pte A. Shaw R.V.C. arrived, having arrived from 3rd M.V.S.	1
	6th		Cpl Earl to Cases 6+9 [?]. Sick and lame by R.T. the lame being brought up to Rabbits with 19 horses for slaughter at LENS H.T. Range B.B.	5
	7th		One J/16 with the transferred Pte Henderson (M.T. driver) admitted to hosp 28 N+R Animal clipped over his hutchy [?] not attended	1
	8th 9th		Animals Cases 6 and 9 sent for burial and destroyed	5
	10th		Day on fin. Ordnance Stores	1
	11th		Motor Ambulance (Closed) for Dunain [?] to left bank ammed	1
	12th		Pte Henderson returned to duty from 87 C.C.S. 49/5/19 Pte [?] for leave	3
	13th		Pte Taber R.A.V.C. reported for duty from [?] [?] attached to the Section from M.V.Sp Anman 2036 [?]. Lost [?] burial by V.S. or R. Motor Ambulance to Dunain [?] for [?]	

Army Form C. 2118.

WAR DIARY
or
INTELLIGENCE SUMMARY.
(Erase heading not required.)

Mobile Veterinary Sec.
No. 1 Area.
No. M.I./44
Date 2/5/19

4 Mobile Vet Summary
Res For
No 1 Area

May 1919

Place	Date	Hour	Summary of Events and Information	Remarks and references to Appendices
ST SAULVE VALENCIENNES	14th		Evacuated 11 animals to No 4 Vety Hospt Galais Loverkerg. Party of 1 Nch 1/c + Pte Pode + Pte Brey draw R.A.V.C. reports & remounts on transfer to this section from 18. V.E.S	Various summary of text 4
	15th-16th		General Duties	
	17th		Waggon (Q.S.) to Orchomis for Stores. Case Book No 35 fold for Butchery + destroyers. Capt Edwards R.A.V.C. No 147 M.V.S. proceeded to Indolers	5
	18th		Capt Pollard R.A.V.C. takes over command of 147 M.V.S. Lt Pollock R.A.V.C. proceeded to Concentration Camp Ben Inlayston. Capt Pride his commander	3
			of Section vice Capt Pollard.	
	19th		Evacuators 6 animals to No 4 Vet Hosp Galais 1/2 of Pte Smith & awaiting (R.S)	1
	20th		Motor Horse Ambulance ambulance to St Ghislain to collect sick animal. Case Book No. 26, 27, 32, 37 fold for Butchery + Destroyers	2
	21st		Waggon (Q.S) for rations 2 days rations on alternate days ammunitions future	
	22nd-23rd		General Duties	
	24th		Waggon Q.S. for fuel + Coal	
	25th		Case Book No 12 + 13 Burnt + for (cache) Knackows to 1st Army Animal Artillery Camp	FMD

May 1918   47th Mobile Veterinary Section

WAR DIARY or INTELLIGENCE SUMMARY

Army Form C. 2118.

(Erase heading not required.)

MOBILE VETERINARY SEC.
No. 1 AREA.
No. M/109
Date 31/5/18

Place	Date	Hour	Summary of Events and Information	Remarks and references to Appendices
ST SAULVE VALENCIENNES	26th		Motor Stores Lorries sent for Repairs to No 1 A.T.M.T. Coy. Pte Henderson M.T. (Armr) proceeded to No 1 A.T.M.T. Coy for demobilization. Pte Proto R.A.S.C.(MT) driver reports for duty to this section from transfer from No 1 A.T.M.T. Coy. Animal No 38 fitted for Butcher & destroyed	Animals admitted for treatment 3
	27th		Waggon (G.S.) to Carriere for Stores	4
	28th		Motor Horse Ambulance despatched to 11 Vet.Ey Regt at station at Antow to collect lame animal. Waggon G.S. to collect Stores at Villers	1
	29th		Evacuated 11 Animals to No 4 V.Ey Hospt Belows. Pte Jackson I/c conducting Party.	1
	30th		Moter ambulance to collect sick + lame animals. Baulk No 47 Mules for Butchery + destroyed. Brought Horses ex Plateau to Sahngo-Dinnop to collect Waggon Box Wheels R.a.S.C.(H.T.) reports for duty to this section on transfer from 2.VI Cavaly Brnvd H.T. Receptn Park	1
	31st		Waggon (G.S.) for fuel + Coal	

W. Butler, Capt. R.A.V.C.
O/c 47 F.M.V.S.

Army Form C. 2118.

WAR DIARY
or
INTELLIGENCE SUMMARY.

47 Mobile Veterinary Section

June 1919

(Erase heading not required.)

Instructions regarding War Diaries and Intelligence Summaries are contained in F.S. Regs., Part II. and the Staff Manual respectively. Title pages will be prepared in manuscript.

Place	Date	Hour	Summary of Events and Information	Remarks and references to Appendices
ST SAULVE	1/6/19		General Duties. Wagon G.S. for rations.	Animals Casualties to M.V.S
VALENCIENNES	2/6/19		General Duties. 2 days rations drawn & attended sick in future	
	3rd		Motor Ambulance (Horse) despatched to 2/3 Bde R.F.A. at Horuchur to collect one animal	
	4th		S.E 25022 Spl Armstrong H.R.A.V.C and 10 Privates sent on duty on transfer from No 13 Veterinary Hospital. Wagon G.S. to Ordinance for stores. Motor Ambulance to Workshops for repairs	
	5th		D.A.D.A.S M.V. Areas visited & inspected the Section	
	6th		SE 113147 Spl Mobile R. 797: Cpl Blackburn J.W. 11848 Pte Cave J.t. 11865 Pte Chappel + 7+ 2 Pte Simes transferred to No 14 No6 Hosp. Bde. Pte Smith J.J R.A.V.C. deposited to No 1 Ameir Remount Squadron horses. Collect 3 animals S.E 32573 Pte Mobile J.S R.A.V.C. reports for duty on transfer from 2/1 (M.L) M.V.S. Wagon G.S. for Bread.	2
	7th		Wagon G.S. with rumors for repair to 9191 Ameir Aux. H.T. Coy. Pte Smith returns from Bourne with 2 animals	
	8th		Horse Hoof Pte Jackson R.A.V.C. Y/c despatched to the Reserve to collect condemned Wagons to O.F.M Josnies	
	9th		General Duties	
	10th		Wagon G.S. to Ordinance for Stores + R.E. Park St Amand. 10 Linn etc Horse Hoof 4t Pte Jackson returns from the Reserve with lame animal Pte Patten R.A.V.C. re-admitted to Reserve to collect animal	1
	11th		M 355213 Pte Patten a R.H.S.E MT No 4 Moto Bank 6" attached to Section for rations + Petrol etc Pte Smith returns from Bourne with a lame animal S.E. 32573 & answer andurece Recoat	2
	19th		General Duties	

O.M Foster Capt R.A.V.C

Army Form C. 2118.

June 1919
47th Mobile V.G
WAR DIARY
or
INTELLIGENCE SUMMARY.
(Erase heading not required.)

47th Mobile
MOBILE VETERINARY
No. 1 AREA.
No. M/204
Date 2nd/7/19

Place	Date	Hour	Summary of Events and Information	Remarks and references to Appendices
ST SAULVE	13/6/19		G.S Limber for Ecole Building for Stores	Animals remaining MV/S 4
VALENCIENNES	14th		Wagon L.S. for Coal + Fuel	
	15th		Case Book No. 49. 1 H.D Horse Note for Butchery	1
			Pte Rogers R.A.V.C. attached to No. 1 Area Remount Reference Horse no. 2 Animals	
	16th		Pte Rogers R.A.V.C. Returns from Loan Case Book No. 551 1 HS Horse Note for Butchery	1
	17 + 18		General Duties	
	19th		169410 3/3 Wheelwright H.R.A.V.C. granted 14 days leave to the United Kingdom from the 20/6/19 to 4/7/19	
	20th		Wagon G.S. to Brunemi for Stores	
	21st		Limber G.S. to Valenciennes sent Below the wounded 3 animals to No.4 Vety Hos and Pts casey + strings	3
	22nd		L.S Wagon for Coal + Fuel	
	23rd		Pte H.E. R.A.V.C. despatcher with Horse Hour to Rennes Convoy cents called Sans animals to No 9 Vet Section Corporal proceeded to the Belfry Valenciennes	
	24th		L.S Wagon. E.N.T.O Ecole Building for Forage	
	25th		General Duties	
	26th		Pte H.W R.A.V.C arrives from Leave - Company report Lame Animal	1
	27th		General Duties	
	28th		Pte Smith + Sparrows R.A.V.C granted 14 days leave to the United Kingdom from 29/6/19 to 13/7/19	
			No 2 D.H 331 Pte Below E York + James R.A.V.C attached to No Unit Waring S Carrier Pul.	
	29th		Pte Garay + Rogers R.A.V.C promoted 14 days leave to the United Kingdom from 30/6/19 to 14/7/19	
	30th		Pte Sealey Tr. + Pte Kelly A.R.A.V.C granted 14 days leave to the United Kingdom from 1/7/19 to 15/7/19	
			T.S/9/BN Farrier TINCLER G R.A.S.C temporarily attached to lu death	

W Foster
Capt R.A.V.C
O/C 47 MVS

Army Form C. 2118.

WAR DIARY
INTELLIGENCE SUMMARY
(Erase heading not required.)

MOBILE VETERINARY SEC. No. 1 AREA.

47th Mobile Veterinary Section
No 1 Area

July 1919

Instructions regarding War Diaries and Intelligence Summaries are contained in F. S. Regs., Part II. and the Staff Manual respectively. Title pages will be prepared in manuscript.

Place	Date	Hour	Summary of Events and Information	Remarks and references to Appendices
St Saulve Valenciennes	1st		31801 Pte Stein R.W.F. proceeded on leave to U.K. from 2/7/19 to 16/7/19. 22573 Pte Nichols R.A.S.C. admitted to 59 C.C.S.	Animals remaining in Sec...
	2-3-4-5-6th		All animals exercised, general duties	
	7th		T/37011 Dvr Roach J. R.A.S.C. reported for duty on transfer from 817th Area H.T. Coy. T/31296 Dvr Mullan S. R.A.S.C. remains G.S. for stores etc. One animal admitted to section. One animal admitted belonging to this section (D.A.D. R.S. & S.)	
	8th		Bdr Brookes G.S. sick (in billets), one animal admitted to section.	
	9th		Dvr Roach J., Pte Williams 1/c of Sec, Allen, dispatched to Beau with 4 horses, formerly the property of P.O.W. Ptes Grierson J. Rave ½c discharged from 352 P.O.W. Coy. Pte Grierson to 353 P.O.W. Coy. One animal admitted to section.	
	10th		Davis Allen & Roach R.A.S.C. return from Beau. One section animal reported deer post mortem (Ruptured liver). Animal admitted to section from Rations for dispatch from 352 P.O.W. C. to Beauvois Bunte Bourne	
	11th		Section vacate the billets at St Saulve & proceed to Beauvois Bunte Bourne.	
Caeron Bunette Bouren	12th		3 animals admitted to Section, General duties	
	13th		229141 Trooper Moores R.W. & Hussars attached to the Section, 3 animals admitted	
	14th		General duties	
	15th		Dvr Roach dispatched with Horse Near K 48 Thomas Rat Cry or ... to ...... collect lame animal	

VIII 114

Army Form C. 2118.

47th Mobile Veterinary Section
No 1 Area

July 1919

WAR DIARY
or
INTELLIGENCE SUMMARY
(Erase heading not required)

47th
MOBILE VETERINARY
SEC.
No. 1 AREA.

Instructions regarding War Diaries and Intelligence Summaries are contained in F.S. Regs., Part II and the Staff Manual respectively. Title pages will be prepared in manuscript.

Place	Date	Hour	Summary of Events and Information	Remarks and references to Appendices
Eastern Frontier District	16th		Cpl Jarvis G + Pte Smart S, Spratt J, Berry J, Willy T + Rogers C RAVC report on return from leave. Lt Unwin R.N., Hanley B.H. Ferguson B. returned from Rly & Vety Hospital duties. Pte Roach returns from duty. Lt Brown rejoins unit. Pte Glasby 76th Labour Coy attached Empanel. 3 animals admitted to R.A.Blan.	
	17th		3 animals admitted to the section.	
	18th		DADVS No 1 Area visited + inspected the section. 2.45pm 21907 Pte Pitney J RAVC returns from leave to HQ UK. 3 animals admitted to the section	
	19th		Pte Pleo J RAVC despatched to Benchant to collect animals from the Trench mullaks. 37018 Bnr Road J Hamilton R 14 AucaHT S.R.A.S.C, T/278418 Dvr Grigman G.W reports for duty on transfer Lo AmcAT/S.R.A.S.C. 32018 Dft/Cpl Brigham J. RAVC + 17923 Pte Jackson W. RASC proceed on 14 days leave to UK whilst Kingston. 30/7/19 to 9/8/19. 3 animals admitted to the section.	
	20th		49247 Pte Skidmore R. 76 Lab Coy report + 12 days sick + is not vety patient to Ex Hollers. Lunt Boyd W + 6P Holler and M Mallen remarked.	
	21st		One animal from M.M.P DSouza admitted as our patient for EMA reshoing	
	22nd		25182 Cpl Armstrong S. proceeds 14 days leave to the United Kingdom from 22/7/19 to 3/8/19 3/72853 Pte Parkes RASC despatched to 14 Base HT Coy for duty. 4 animals admitted to the section.	
	23rd		Pte Blakmer 76th Lab Coy despatched to his unit. 9 animals + 20 Horse Mails W.C. Pte Trap W RAVC despatched to No 14 Veterinary Hospl Galon + Sare Brok W.G by Peter for Bullion Sundry of BADV Khartoum	
	24th		2nd Multan S RASC despatched with animal G.S. Cruise (2 ptles) an animal from 14 Green admitted as our patient for FwH reshoing	
	25th		One animal from 2071/4 OhOAHT S/7 Loy admitted as our patient for FwH reshoing	

Army Form C. 2118.

July 1919 47 Mobile Veterinary Section
No. 1 Area

WAR DIARY
or
INTELLIGENCE SUMMARY.
(Erase heading not required)

47th MOBILE VETERINARY SEC. NO. I AREA.

Place	Date	Hour	Summary of Events and Information	Remarks and references to Appendices
Bourre Ruvelle	26th		S.Q.B. M/S. M.V.S. No 1 Amb. marches + two section sections. Two animals admitted to section.	
Douai	27th		SE 14416 S/S Robinson S. Reece reports for duty on transfer from No 11 Veterinary Hosp. Calais. Para Book No. 50 Buried + returned to H.Q. Aux H.T. B.M.	
	28th		One Animal from 14 Aux HT B.M. suffering from bombard skin trouble as out patient.	
	29th		SE 28836 Pte Furguson J.R. granted 14 days leave to the United Kingdom. One animal admitted to the Section. Para Book No. 61 Para Book No 62 for Burying	
	30th		Para Book 66 buried + returned to Unit + Para Book No. 67, 71, 72 buried + returned to Units	
	31st		1290 S/S Whitmarsh S.R. Q.V.C. reports after being 25 days absent without leave in the U.K. Remanded for Cond Mr. Co. Para Book No. 701 buried + returned to Unit	

C.W. Foster Lieut.
O.C. 47 M.V.S.

B
Aug
1919
Mehring

Army Form C. 2118.

WAR DIARY
or
INTELLIGENCE SUMMARY.
(Erase heading not required.)

Instructions regarding War Diaries and Intelligence Summaries are contained in F. S. Regs., Part II. and the Staff Manual respectively. Title pages will be prepared in manuscript.

WAR DIARY of No. 47 MOBILE VETERINARY SECTION.

Place	Date	Hour	Summary of Events and Information	Remarks and references to Appendices
DOUAI.	1st September.	"	Routine Work.	
	2nd	"	Lame animal collected from VALENCIENNES.	
	3rd.	"	Two animals admitted as Out Patients from "Z" Horse Depot for teeth rasping.	
	4th	"	One animal collected by Float from BETHUNE. One animal received from No. 14 Army Aux. Horse Coy. S/S. ROBINSON. Ptes. JACKSON SPROSON sent to VALENCIENNES for demobilization.	
	5th.	"	L/Cpl. BRAYSHAW proceeds to VALENCIENNES to provide escort for S/SWHEELWRIGHT who returns to duty on completion of 21 days Field Punishment No. ".	
	6th.	"	Pte. WEBSTER discharged from No. 6 Casualty Clearing Station and returns to duty.	
	7th	"	Routine Work.	
	8th	"	Pte. MOORE attached 47 M.V.S. granted 14 days leave to United Kingdom. Two animals admitted from "Z" Horse Depot.	
	9th.	"	Case Book No. 85 cured and returned to Unit in charge of Pte. KELLY.	
	10th	"	Two animals admitted from 14 Army Aux. Transport Coy. Two animals sold to Butcher.	
	11th	"	Pte. WEBSTER despatched to VALENCIENNES to collect sick animal. One animal sold to Butcher.	
	12th	"	Routine work.	
	13th	"	Routine work.	
	14th	"	Three sick animals admitted from "Z" Horse Depot.	

Army Form C. 2118.

WAR DIARY
or
INTELLIGENCE SUMMARY.
(Erase heading not required.)

Instructions regarding War Diaries and Intelligence Summaries are contained in F. S. Regs., Part II. and the Staff Manual respectively. Title pages will be prepared in manuscript.

Place	Date	Hour	Summary of Events and Information	Remarks and references to Appendices
DOUAI.	15th September.		Captain A.N.FOSTER., O.B.E. proceeds on leave to U.K. Duties carried out by Major T. HIBBARD., D.A.D.V.S. No. 1 AREA. Pte. WEBSTER proceeds on leave to U.K. S/S.WHEELWRIGHT and Pte. WILLIAMS despatched to No. 4 Veterinary Hospital for demobilization.	
	16th		Eight Other Ranks received from No. 4 Veterinary Hospital to bring strength of Mobile Veterinary Section to Establishment.	
	17th.		Routine work.	
	18th.		Routine work.	
	19th.		Section visited by Colonel W.A.PALLIN. D.D.V.S., British Troops in France & Flanders.	
	20th.		Sgt. BROOM. R.A.V.C. attached to No. 47 Mobile Veterinary Section for temporary duty. Cpl. ARMSTRONG despatched to P.O.W. Staging Camp CAMBRAI to collect surplus animals.	
	21st		Pte. ROGERS 1/c. and two Other Ranks despatched to CAMBRAI to collect surplus animals.	
	22nd		Thirty seven animals admitted to be disposed of by Sale. One animal sold to Butcher.	
	23rd.		Dvr. NUTTALL R.A.S.C. granted 14 days leave to U.K. Three sick animals admitted from 14 Army Aux. Horse Coy. Nine animals received from CAMBRAI to be disposed of by Sale.	
	24th		Pte. KELLY 1/c and two Other Ranks proceed to CAMBRAI to collect surplus animals. Twenty-one animals admitted from CAMBRAI to be disposed of by Sale.	
	25th		Eight animals sold to Butcher. Thirteen sick animals admitted from "Z" Horse Depot. Twelve surplus animals received from CAMBRAI for Sale.	
	26th		Pte. ROGERS 1/c and two Other Ranks proceed to CAMBRAI to collect surplus animals. Seventeen surplus animals received from CAMBRAI for Sale.	
	27th		Seventy One animals sold to Farmers etc. from No. 47 Mobile Veterinary Section. Fifteen animals received from CAMBRAI.	

Army Form C. 2118.

WAR DIARY
or
INTELLIGENCE SUMMARY.
(Erase heading not required.)

Instructions regarding War Diaries and Intelligence Summaries are contained in F. S. Regs., Part II. and the Staff Manual respectively. Title pages will be prepared in manuscript.

Place	Date	Hour	Summary of Events and Information	Remarks and references to Appendices
DOUAI.	28th September.		Pte. ROGER 1/c and two Other Ranks despatched to CAMBRAI to collect surplus animals. Fifteen animals received from CAMBRAI.	
	29th.	"	Sgt HUGHES reports for duty on transfer from No. 4 Veterinary Hospital CALAIS. Sgt. BROOM returned to Unit. Received twenty three animals from CAMBRAI for Sale. One animal sold to Butcher. Charger of Captain A.N.FOSTER died. *Section studies*	
	30th.	"	Post Mortem of charger of Captain A.N.FOSTER. Diagnosis: Ruptured diaphragm. Pte. TOPP 1/c and two Other Ranks despatched to CAMBRAI to collect surplus animals. Nineteen animals received from CAMBRAI. Five animals sold to Butcher.	

DOUAI.
October 7th, 1919.

[signature]
Captain.
S.V.O. No. 1 DISTRICT.

C
sept 1919
Duplicated

Army Form C. 2118.

WAR DIARY
or
INTELLIGENCE SUMMARY.
(Erase heading not required.)

Instructions regarding War Diaries and Intelligence Summaries are contained in F. S. Regs., Part II. and the Staff Manual respectively. Title pages will be prepared in manuscript.

Place	Date	Hour	Summary of Events and Information	Remarks and references to Appendices

WAR DIARY of No. 47 MOBILE VETERINARY SECTION.

DOUAI.

	1st September.		Routine Work.
	2nd "		Lame animal collected from VALENCIENNES.
	3rd. "		Two animals admitted as Out Patients from "Z" Horse Depot for teeth rasping.
	4th "		One animal collected by Float from BETHUNE. One animal received from No. 14 Army Aux. Horse Coy. S/S. ROBINSON. Ptes. JACKSON SPROSON sent to VALENCIENNES for demobilization.
	5th. "		L/Cpl. BRAYSHAW proceeds to VALENCIENNES to provide escort for S/SWHEELWRIGHT who returns to duty on completion of 21 days Field Punishment No. "
	6th. "		Pte. WEBSTER discharged from No. 6 Casualty Clearing Station and returns to duty.
	7th "		Routine Work.
	8th "		Pte. MOORE attached 47 M.V.S. granted 14 days leave to United Kingdom. Two animals admitted from "Z" Horse Depot.
	9th. "		Case Book No. 85 cured and returned to Unit in charge of Pte. KELLY.
	10th "		Two animals admitted from 14 Army Aux. Transport Coy. Two animals sold to Butcher.
	11th "		Pte. WEBSTER despatched to VALENCIENNES to collect sick animal. One animal sold to Butcher.
	12th "		Routine work.
	13th "		Routine work.
	14th "		Three sick animals admitted from "Z" Horse Depot.

AW Foster Capt.

Army Form C. 2118.

WAR DIARY
or
INTELLIGENCE SUMMARY.
(Erase heading not required.)

Instructions regarding War Diaries and Intelligence Summaries are contained in F. S. Regs., Part II. and the Staff Manual respectively. Title pages will be prepared in manuscript.

Remarks and references to Appendices

A.N. Foster. Capt.

Place	Date	Hour	Summary of Events and Information
DOUAI.	15th September.		Captain A.N. FOSTER., O.B.E. proceeds on leave to U.K. Duties carried out by Major T. HIBBARD., D.A.D.V.S. No. 1 AREA. Pte. WEBSTER proceeds on leave to U.K. S/S.WHEELWRIGHT and Pte. WILLIAMS despatched to No. 4 Veterinary Hospital for demobilization.
	16th	"	Eight Other Ranks received from No. 4 Veterinary Hospital to bring strength of Mobile Veterinary Section to Establishment.
	17th.	"	Routine work.
	18th	"	Routine work.
	19th.	"	Section visited by Colonel W.A. PALLIN. D.D.V.S., British Troops in France & Flanders.
	20th.	"	Sgt. BROOM. R.A.V.C. attached to No. 47 Mobile Veterinary Section for temporary duty. Cpl. ARMSTRONG despatched to P.O.W. Staging Camp CAMBRAI to collect surplus animals.
	21st	"	Pte. ROGERS 1/c. and two Other Ranks despatched to CAMBRAI to collect surplus animals.
	22nd	"	Thirty seven animals admitted to be disposed of by Sale. One animal sold to Butcher.
	23rd.	"	Dvr. NUTTALL R.A.S.C. granted 14 days leave to U.K. Three sick animals admitted from 14 Army Aux. Horse Coy. Nine animals received from CAMBRAI to be disposed of by Sale.
	24th.	"	Pte. KELIY 1/c and two Other Ranks proceed to CAMBRAI to collect surplus animals. Twenty-one animals admitted from CAMBRAI to be disposed of by Sale.
	25th	"	Eight animals sold to Butcher. Thirteen sick animals admitted from "Z" Horse Depot. Twelve surplus animals received from CAMBRAI for Sale.
	26th	"	Pte. ROGERS 1/c and two Other Ranks proceed to CAMBRAI to collect surplus animals. Seventeen surplus animals received from CAMBRAI for Sale.
	27th	"	Seventy One animals sold to Farmers etc. from No. 47 Mobile Veterinary Section. Fifteen animals received from CAMBRAI.

Army Form C. 2118.

WAR DIARY
or
INTELLIGENCE SUMMARY.
(Erase heading not required.)

Instructions regarding War Diaries and Intelligence Summaries are contained in F. S. Regs., Part II. and the Staff Manual respectively. Title pages will be prepared in manuscript.

Place	Date	Hour	Summary of Events and Information	Remarks and references to Appendices
DOUAI.	28th September.		Pte. ROGER 1/c and two Other Ranks despatched to CAMBRAI to collect surplus animals. Fifteen animals received from CAMBRAI.	
	29th.	"	Sgt HUGHES reports for duty on transfer from No. 4 Veterinary Hospital CALAIS. Sgt. BROOM returned to Unit. Received twenty three animals from CAMBRAI for sale. One animal sold to Butcher. Charger of Captain A.N.FOSTER dies. *Section Rider*	
	30th	"	Post Mortem of charger of Captain A.N.FOSTER. Diagnosis: Ruptured diaphragm. Pte. TOPP 1/c and two Other Ranks despatched to CAMBRAI to collect surplus animals. Nineteen animals received from CAMBRAI. Five animals sold to Butcher.	

DOUAI.
October 7th, 1919.

A.N. Foster
Captain.
S.V.O. No. 1 DISTRICT.

No. 1 District No. 12 Q.

D. A. & Q. M. G.,
   (Record Section).
     British Troops in France & Flanders.

    The attached Veterinary Summary for No. 1 District for the month of October 1919 is forwarded.

Headquarters.
No. 1 District.
 // Nov. 1919.
                                       Colonel.
                          Commanding No. 1 District.

FHW.

"Q" BRANCH H.Q.
No. 120
Date 10-11-19

47th MOBILE VETERINARY SEC. No. 1 AREA
No. MV 614
Date 8/11/19

D.A.Q.M.G.
H.Q. N.I. District.

Reference my N.I. 598 of 4/11/19 & accompanying summary & your acknowledgement thereof — will you kindly forward to Record Section G.H.Q. — I take it that I am to forward it direct to them in future.

Caserne Dumitte
Douai.

A.H. Foster. Capt.
S.V.O. N.I. District

Army Form C. 2118.

WAR DIARY / INTELLIGENCE SUMMARY.
(Erase heading not required.)

Veterinary N. District -
and including
4 Mobile Veterinary Section.

October 1919.

Condition & General Health of animals of N. District has been satisfactory during the month. No outbreak of Contagious Disease has occurred. One thousand & thirty eight (1,038) animals have been disposed of by Public Auction during the month. Seven sales have been held at Douai. One sale has been held at Valenciennes. Prices for animals at Valenciennes were well maintained and it is proposed to hold further sales at this place. Prices for animals of Douai have been well maintained and it's not prohibitive sale should be held this. Two hundred four Animals have been disposed of for Butcher during the month. One hundred fifty eight (158) of these have been sent by road to Lille. The remaining 46 have been sold to Butchers in and around Douai. Specific ophthalmia and it's sequels have caused the greatest number of animals to fall into the Butcher class. Wounds - Cellulitis account for a few cases - old age - Debility - Lameness

Sheet 2:

Army Form C. 2118.

WAR DIARY
INTELLIGENCE SUMMARY

(Erase heading not required.)

Veterinary No 1 District including 47 Mobile Veterinary Section

Place	Date	Hour	Summary of Events and Information	Remarks and references to Appendices
	October 1919.			

Sidgeone.

From Ringbone there has only been a very small factor in determining the animals should be classed for Butchery :- By Public Auction has been subjected to All animals sold for Butchery & Public Auction are thoroughly the Mallein Test and not one animal has reacted :- All animals sold by Public Auction are thoroughly satisfactorily. The has been a good demand for W.D, L.D, and Mules - Riders & Horses generally of poor stamp are not much sought after.-

On the 30th of this month - two personnel of 47. M.V.S. underwents. Complete Change :- A draft of veterinary other ranks was posted from the Base and demobilitate personnel was sent to No 4 Veterinary Hospital Calais. Number

The smallness of Personnel & the large numbers of animals &c. handled render our growing impracticable.— the lack of clerical assistance renders it difficult to render returns & keep correspondence up to date.—

MOBILE VETERINARY SEC.
No. 1 AREA
47th

Officer i/c R.A.V.C.
    Records.
      Woolwich
        London. S.E.

The attached duplicate copy of Summary of 4. Mobile Veterinary Section for the month of September 1919. is forwarded to you please ---

H.Q.
Forward Districts:-
3 - 12 - 1919.

A.M. Foster. Major.
D.A.D.V.S.
Forward Districts.

Army Form C. 2118.

WAR DIARY
INTELLIGENCE SUMMARY.
(Erase heading not required.)

Veterinary N°1 District
474 Mobile Veterinary Section:-

Place	Date	Hour	Summary of Events and Information	Remarks and references to Appendices
			Period 1 – 24 November 1919.	

Condition & General Health of animals of N°1 District has been satisfactory during the month:- No outbreak of Contagious Disease has occurred –
One hundred & fifty three animals surplus to the requirements of the army have been disposed of by Public Auction during the month:- Two sales having been held at Douai:-
Prices of animals have been well maintained, the average price for all Classes of animals, having been over twelve hundred francs each:-
Sick animals have been sold for Butchers during the Month, locally, in Douai:- The largest number falls into the Butchers Class owing to Specific Ophthalmia in its effect:- Ulcerative Cellulitis, determines the late of a few and a certain number of animals have to be destroyed on account of Debility, of say, Lameness arising from Ringbone; Exhibitor – All animals admitted to 2 Horse Depôt of Casting, though 474 M.V.S., 30 epi: have been subjected to the Mallein Test & not a single reactor has occurred.

51. M.V.S. arrived Douai 21-11-19

Sheet 2.

WAR DIARY
Veterinary No. 1 Dist'n including 47 Mobile Veterinary Section
INTELLIGENCE SUMMARY.
(Erase heading not required.)

Army Form C. 2118.

Place	Date	Hour	Summary of Events and Information	Remarks and references to Appendices
	October 1919		Dehlili. Lameness from Ring bone Ricketone have only been a very small factor in determining that animals should be cleared for Butchery. All animals sold for Butchery by Public Auction have been Subjected to the Mallein Test and not one animal has reacted:- All animals sold by Public Auction are thoroughly serviceable + their has been a good demand for H.D.L.D. and Mules. Riders which are generally of poor stamp are not much sought after:- On the 30th of this month – the Personnel of 47 M.V.S. underwent a complete change:- a draft of detainable other ranks was posted from the Base and demobilizable Personnel was sent to No. 14 Veterinary Hospital:- The sudden number of Personnel The large numbers of animals to be handled render grooming impracticable:- The lack of clerical assistance renders it difficult to render returns and keep correspondence up to date ———	

Sheet. 3

WAR DIARY
INTELLIGENCE SUMMARY.

Veterinary Nº 1 District Army Form C. 2118.
including
47 Mobile Veterinary Section

Place	Date	Hour	Summary of Events and Information	Remarks and references to Appendices
47th MOBILE VETERINARY SEC. NO. 1 AREA.			October 1919 Correspondence is much delayed en route — owing one assumes to reduced postal service — lack of transport other than horses makes it impossible to visit and inspect units which are far afield :— A.W. Foster Captain. S.O. Nº 1 District.	

Sheet 3.

Army Form C. 2118.

WAR DIARY

INTELLIGENCE SUMMARY.

(Erase heading not required.)

Veterinary N°. 1 District
relieving
#7 Mobile Veterinary Section

October 1919.

Instructions regarding War Diaries and Intelligence Summaries are contained in F. S. Regs., Part II. and the Staff Manual respectively. Title pages will be prepared in manuscript.

Place	Date	Hour	Summary of Events and Information	Remarks and references to Appendices
			Correspondence is much delayed or lost :- owing one assumes to reduced postal service. - Lack of transport other than horses makes it impossible to visit and inspect units which are far afield :-	

A.M. Foster. Captain.
S.V.O. N°.1 District.

47706
MOBILE VETERINARY
SEC.
NO. 1 AREA

No.
Date

> 47th
> MOBILE VETERINARY
> SEC.
> No. I AREA.
>
> No. 4 R S
> Date 25/11/19

Herewith Intelligence Summary
Veterinary N° 1 District by M.V.S.
for 1 - 25 November 1919 (period)

Kindly acknowledge receipt to
D.A.D.V.S. Forward District.

[signature] Capt.
R.A.V.C.

WAR DIARY or **INTELLIGENCE SUMMARY.** Veterinary N. District 47th Mobile Veterinary Section.

Army Form C. 2118.

Place	Date	Hour	Summary of Events and Information	Remarks and references to Appendices
			November 1 - 25 - 1919	

Condition & General Health of animals of N. District has been satisfactory during the month. No outbreak of Contagious Disease has occurred. One hundred & fifty three animals surplus to the requirements of the Army have been disposed of by Public Auction during the month. Wholesale have been rather lower. - Prices of animals have been well maintained - the average price of Classes of animals having been over twelve hundred francs each. - Sick Animals have been sold for Butchery during the period twenty Drawi:- the largest number of animals fall to the Butcher, claiming to Specific Ophthalmus & its effects - Weather conditions determines the fate of a fair & small number of animals have to be destroyed on account of Debility & old age - Lameness arising from Ringbone - Confirmed Cribbiters have also been sold for Butchery:- Animals admitted to R. Horse Depot & those passing through 47. M.V.S. have been subjected to the Mallein Test & not a single reaction has occurred. -

A.H. Foster, Capt.

Army Form C. 2118.

WAR DIARY
or
INTELLIGENCE SUMMARY.
(Erase heading not required.)

Veterinary N⁰ 1 District
947. Mobile Veterinary Section.

Place	Date	Hour	Summary of Events and Information	Remarks and references to Appendices
Veterinary N⁰ 1 District	1–25 November 1919		51. M.V.S. arrived in Donai 21-11-19. S.V.O. visited N⁰ 1 District 21-11-19. 47. M.V.S. was finally broken up on 24-11-19. Ordnance Stores & Equipment were sent to Divisionen 22/11/19. Horses were transferred to 51. M.V.S. 23-11-19. Personnel of 47. M.V.S. was transferred to 51. M.V.S. & N⁰ 4 Veterinary Hospital on 24-11-19. Completion of breaking up 47. M.V.S. was reported to O.S.V.S. 8V.S. & V.S. 8% 5. H.Q. 1 District. Senior Veterinary Officer N⁰ 1 District. Those duties are assumed by Captain A.S. Meeks R.A.V.C. from 24/11/19. Clearing up Inspection & Removal of 47. M.V.S. will be completed on 26/11/19. Proceed on 24/11/19 to S.R. Rot Transume duties of S.V.O.V.S. forward district.	

A.L. Doctor Captain:
R.A.V.C.

WAR DIARY
INTELLIGENCE SUMMARY

Army Form C. 2118.

Veterinary No. 1 District. #7 Mobile Veterinary Section

D.D.V.S. Visited No. 1 District 21-11-19:-

#7. M.V.S. was taken up on 24-11-19:- Ordnance Stores were sent to Advance on 22/11/19:- Horses were transferred to 57. M.V.S. 23/11/19. Personnel was transferred to 4 Veterinary Hospital & 51. M.V.S. on 24/11/19:- Completion of Instructions issued was reported to D.D.V.S. B9 in. Lgs. No 1. District on 25-11-19:-

From 24-11-19: Captain A.V. Meeke takes over duties of S.V.O. No 1 District & on clearing up Records of #7 M.V.S. proceed to base D.A.D.V.S. forward destricks:- on 27-4-19.

A.V. Foster, Captain
R.A.V.C.

www.ingramcontent.com/pod-product-compliance
Lightning Source LLC
Chambersburg PA
CBHW080856230426
43662CB00013B/2116